D0390096

HE GAVE GIFTS

BIBLE STUDY GUIDE

From the Bible-teaching ministry of

Charles R. Swindoll

INSIGHT FOR LIVING

Charles R. Swindoll is a graduate of Dallas Theological Seminary and has served as senior pastor of the First Evangelical Free Church of Fullerton, California, since 1971. Chuck's radio program, "Insight for Living," began in 1979. In addition to his church and radio ministries, Chuck enjoys writing. He has authored numerous books and booklets on a variety of subjects.

Based on the outlines and transcripts of Chuck's sermons, the study guide text is co-authored by Bryce Klabunde, a graduate of Biola University and Dallas Theological Seminary. He also wrote the Living Insights sections.

Editor in Chief:
Cynthia Swindoll

Coauthor of Text:
Bryce Klabunde

Assistant Editor:
Wendy Peterson

Copy Editors:
Ellen Galey,
Glenda Schlahta

Production Artist:
Cindy Ford

Typographer:
Bob Haskins

Director, Communications Division:
Deedee Snyder

Project Manager:
Alene Cooper

Project Coordinator:
Susan Nelson

Assistant Print Production Manager:
John Norton

Printer:
Frye and Smith

Unless otherwise identified, all Scripture references are from the New American Standard Bible, © The Lockman Foundation 1960, 1962, 1963, 1968, 1971, 1972, 1973, 1975, 1977. Used by permission. Scripture taken from the Holy Bible, New International Version, Copyright © 1973, 1978, 1984 International Bible Society, used by permission of Zondervan Bible Publishers. Other translations cited are the King James Version of the Bible [KJV], the New King James Version [NKJV], and J.B. Phillips: The New Testament in Modern English [PHILLIPS].

© 1992 Charles R. Swindoll. All rights reserved.

Outlines and transcripts:
© 1991 Charles R. Swindoll. All rights reserved.

An effort has been made to locate sources and obtain permission where necessary for the quotations used in this book. In the event of any unintentional omission, a modification will gladly be incorporated in future printings.

Notice

No portion of this publication may be translated into any language or reproduced in any form, except for brief quotations in reviews, without prior written permission of the publisher, Insight for Living, Post Office Box 69000, Anaheim, California 92817-0900.

ISBN 0-8499-8431-9

Printed in the United States of America.

COVER DESIGN: Diana Vasquez

CONTENTS

INTRODUCTION

Some scriptual studies are interesting and invigorating. Others are reassuring and comforting. On a few, rare occasions, however, we come across a study that is downright life-changing. This is such a study.

I'm being honest with you when I say that this series on the spiritual gifts in the body of Christ can literally transform your life. When I first came to terms with this subject, I discovered the gift(s) God had given me . . . and I was immediately relieved of needless guilt because I wasn't doing *more and more* things for God. I found great satisfaction in knowing that the Lord had given me certain abilities and my responsibility was to carry them out through His power and for His glory.

My great hope is that you and every other person who goes through the series with us will dig into this study with unusual zeal. Why? So that all may come to realize how and where God has gifted them so that the numerous needs in the body may be met. As we undertake an in-depth analysis of the spiritual gifts, let's pray—fervently pray—that eyes and hearts will be open to new and unexpected truth. The fact is, you may never be quite the same once you have been exposed to this teaching and have begun exercising your gifts. Exciting thought, isn't it?

Chuck Swindoll

Chuck Swindoll

PUTTING TRUTH
INTO ACTION

Knowledge apart from application falls short of God's desire for His children. He wants us to apply what we learn so that we will change and grow. This study guide was prepared with these goals in mind. As you go through the following pages, we hope your desire to discover biblical truth will grow as your understanding of God's Word increases, and that you will be encouraged to apply what you've learned.

To assist you in your study, we've included a section called Living Insights at the end of each lesson. These exercises will challenge you to study further and to think of specific ways to put your discoveries into action.

There are many ways to use this guide—in personal devotions, group studies, discussions with friends and family, and Sunday school classes. And, of course, it's an ideal study aid when you're listening to its corresponding "Insight for Living" radio series.

To benefit most from this study guide, we would encourage you to consider it a spiritual journal. That's why we've included space in the Living Insights for recording your thoughts and discoveries. We hope you'll return to those sections often for review and encouragement as you continue to grow in your walk with Christ.

Bryce Klabunde

Bryce Klabunde
Coauthor of Text
Author of Living Insights

HE GAVE
GIFTS

Chapter 1

HE GAVE GIFTS

Selected Scripture

During the Great Depression, poverty swept across America like a whirling tornado, ripping up dreams and scattering hopes to the wind. One such poverty twister hit a small part of Texas where a man named Yates ran a sheep ranch. Struggling even to keep food on the table, Yates and his wife did all they could to survive. Finally, they had to accept a government subsidy or lose their home and land to the creditors.

One day, in the midst of this bleakness, a geologic crew from a large oil company came knocking. With Yates' permission, they wanted to drill a wildcat well on his property, promising him a large portion of the profits if they struck oil. "What could I lose?" thought Yates, and he signed all the papers.

The oil crew immediately set up the machinery and began drilling. Five hundred feet down, they came up dry. Eight hundred feet, still dry. One thousand feet they sunk the shaft, and no oil. Finally, at a little over eleven hundred feet, they tapped into one of the richest oil reserves in Texas. The hole sprayed its black wealth high into the air, and soon the well was pumping eighty thousand barrels of oil a day.

Overnight, Yates and his family became millionaires. His property, once called Yates' Field, became known as Yates' Pool. And soon hundreds of oil wells dotted the land where once only sheep grazed.[1]

Here was a man who all along had the potential to make millions yet, in the beginning, lived on welfare. Amazing. But if you think about it, many of us Christians are just like him. We struggle along

---

1. Based on a story told by Bill Bright in *How You Can Be Filled with the Holy Spirit* (Arrowhead Springs, Calif.: New Life 2000 Publications, 1991), pp. 28–29.

at the spiritual poverty level, unaware of the vast resources God has placed in our possession. For out of His bounty, God has given each of us a plentiful reserve in the form of spiritual gifts. In the lessons that follow, we'll be drilling into our pools of spiritual gifts to discover their limitless potential to enrich our Christian lives.

Our exploration begins in 1 Corinthians 12, where the apostle Paul provides us with some essential background about spiritual gifts.

> Now concerning spiritual gifts, brethren, I do not want you to be unaware.[2] . . .
> . . . There are varieties of gifts, but the same Spirit. And there are varieties of ministries, and the same Lord. And there are varieties of effects, but the same God who works all things in all persons. But to each one is given the manifestation of the Spirit for the common good. (vv. 1, 4–7)

Three facts concerning spiritual gifts stand out in these verses. First, the Holy Spirit distributes a *variety of gifts*. Simply because one Spirit is doing the giving doesn't mean that He has only one gift to give. No, His resources are limitless and His creativity infinite. Also, believers can exercise their gifts to accomplish a *variety of ministries*. The wide array of gifts has an equally broad spectrum of ministries to match. And finally, when you utilize your gifts, a *variety of effects* benefit the body of Christ. All of this wonderful variety converges into one overarching purpose: "the common good."

In his letter to the Ephesians, Paul highlights another facet of this spiritual gifts treasure.

> But to *each* one of us grace was given according to the measure of Christ's gift. Therefore it says,
> "When He ascended on high,
> He led captive a host of captives,[3]
> And He gave gifts to men."
> (4:7–8, emphasis added)

---

2. Paul mentions three aspects of the Christian life of which he particularly wants the believer to be aware—first, Satan and his schemes (2 Cor. 2:11); second, death and the afterlife (1 Thess. 4:13–18); and third, our present subject of spiritual gifts.

3. For more information about what happened between Christ's resurrection and ascension, see Robert A. Morey's book *Death and the Afterlife* (Minneapolis, Minn.: Bethany House Publishers, 1984), pp. 85–86.

"To each one of us . . . He gave gifts"! This means that *every* believer, even on a bad day, has a never-ending reserve of Christ's kingly gifts. For our Christ is indeed a King, ascended to heaven and enthroned beside the Father, graciously gifting the subjects He has redeemed.

Definition: What Is a "Spiritual Gift"?

This initial examination opens a broad vista concerning spiritual gifts. Now let's focus on the specific features of this terrain.

Original Meaning of the Terms

Simply stated, a spiritual gift is *a skill or an ability that enables each Christian to perform a function in the body of Christ with ease and effectiveness.* It is given by the Lord, it's spiritual in kind, and it's something that comes easily. Like adding the missing piece to a puzzle, when we put our gift into action, the whole body of believers benefits. Consequently, our greatest, most effective contribution to other Christians is to exercise our gift.

Practical Meaning of the Truth

Acting on our gift takes a course much like Mr. Yates' discovery of oil. There he was, sitting on his front porch, contemplating his troubles, completely unaware that the solution was flowing right below him. He needed someone else to tap him on the shoulder and say, "Friend, you're sittin' on millions!" And once he heard the good news, he needed to drill right away.

In the same way, the lessons in this study will tap you on the shoulder and inform you about God's riches underneath the surface in your life. When they do, drop a shaft into the pool, and begin enjoying the payoff your spiritual gift brings to your life and the lives of others. As Paul encouraged Timothy, "Stir up the gift of God which is in you" (2 Tim. 1:6 NKJV).

Questions: What Are the Crucial Issues?

You may be saying, "Yes, I do want to know more about my spiritual gift," but you still may have some questions that need answering before you can explore your gift much further. So let's address some of these crucial issues, using the greatest Sourcebook available—the Bible.

Are Spiritual Gifts and the Gift of the Holy Spirit the Same?

Spiritual gifts are far different from the gift of the Holy Spirit in that spiritual gifts are abilities or skills, while the gift of the Holy Spirit is a Person—the third member of the Trinity. Let's take a moment to acquaint ourselves with Him through Jesus' letter of introduction.

> "And I will ask the Father, and He will give you another Helper, that He may be with you forever; that is the Spirit of truth, whom the world cannot receive, because it does not behold Him or know Him, but you know Him because He abides with you, and will be in you. I will not leave you as orphans. . . .
>
> ". . . But the Helper, the Holy Spirit, whom the Father will send in My name, He will teach you all things, and bring to your remembrance all that I said to you." (John 14:16–18, 26)

Always loving and mindful of our needs, Jesus and the Father gave us a gift: the gift of their presence, the Holy Spirit. "I will not leave you as orphans," Jesus assured, and He graciously provided One who would come beside us to help us live our new lives in Christ.

As the Helper, the Holy Spirit plays an important role concerning spiritual gifts.

Who Gives the "Gifts of the Spirit"?

God gives the Holy Spirit, and, according to the following verses, the Holy Spirit gives the gifts.

> But to each one is given the manifestation of the Spirit for the common good. . . . But one and the same Spirit works all these things, distributing to each one individually just as He wills. (1 Cor. 12:7, 11)

Notice that the Holy Spirit's distribution of spiritual gifts is "just as He wills." This means that we don't need to pray, plead, or wait for our gift. We should be wary of anyone who teaches that we can acquire spiritual gifts through self-effort. In fact, the opposite is true, for the Holy Spirit matches us with our gift *without* any effort on our part. And it's always a perfect fit.

The Holy Spirit gives the gifts, but some may consider their Christian lives and reflect, "I don't feel like I have a special gift

4

from the Lord. Could the Holy Spirit have missed me somehow?" That feeling brings us to our next question.

Is It True That Every Christian Has at Least One Gift?

Does *every* Christian, without exception, have at least one spiritual gift? The answer to this question is a reassuring yes. To make the point clear, Paul repeats a crucial phrase in his teaching on the gifts: *"each one* is given the manifestation of the Spirit" (v. 7); "the same Spirit . . . distributing to *each one* individually" (v. 11); and "God has placed the members, *each one* of them, in the body" (v. 18). Each believer has a gift (see also Eph. 4:7), and some may even have more than one.

What exactly are these gifts each one of us has?

Are There Lists of Spiritual Gifts in the Bible?

Six passages in the Bible discuss spiritual gifts, and the following chart provides a listing of them for you.[4]

New Testament Lists of Spiritual Gifts		
1 Corinthians 12:8–10	*1 Corinthians 12:28*	*1 Corinthians 12:29–30*
Word of wisdom	Apostleship	Apostleship
Word of knowledge	Prophecy	Prophecy
Faith	Teaching	Teaching
Healing	Miracles	Miracles
Miracles	Healing	Healing
Prophecy	Helps	Tongues
Distinguishing of spirits	Administrating	Interpreting tongues
Tongues	Tongues	
Interpreting tongues		
Romans 12:6–8	*Ephesians 4:11*	*1 Peter 4:11*
Prophecy	Apostleship	Speaking
Serving	Prophecy	Serving
Teaching	Evangelism	
Exhorting	Pastor-Teacher	
Giving		
Leading		
Showing mercy		

4. This chart is adapted from William McRae's *Dynamics of Spiritual Gifts* (Grand Rapids, Mich.: Zondervan Publishing House, 1976), p. 44.

The lists are amazing—and the possibilities are exciting, aren't they? But for all the excitement, one little nagging question threatens to darken our hearts: Can we lose a gift? Paul calms our spirits with his reassuring words, "The gifts and the calling of God are irrevocable" (Rom. 11:29). Even if we are unaware of our gift or fail to exercise it or fall into sin? Even then. *Irrevocable.*

If God has given us such lasting and valuable treasures, how do we find out more about them? How do we even know which ones are ours?

How Can I Discover Which Gift Is Mine?

The first step to discovering your spiritual gift is to *be informed.* Study each of the gifts, and ask yourself—and others—which ones may apply to you.

The next step is to *be open,* for your gift may be different than you think. Allow the Lord—and others—to help you discover your gift.

Third, *be available.* Try a variety of gifts, and see how they fit.

Finally, *be sensitive* to the feedback you receive from others. Pay attention to the responses of others and to your own feelings in this process. When you expressed this gift, was it enjoyable? Effective? Did it come easily?

Suggestions: What Difference Does It Make?

As we have traveled from verse to verse in this first lesson, we hope that we've answered some of your questions. One vital issue remains, however: What difference does it make for me to use my gift? What would happen if I didn't use my gift?

First, if you leave your gift on the shelf, you will never experience all that the Lord wants to do through you. And second, you will always wonder, Is my present life fulfilling God's purpose for me?

Only by using your gift can you release the marvelous, powerful workings of God that await you. When this happens, God will reveal to you a ministry and purpose for life that perfectly matches your abilities and skills.

So through the next nine chapters of this study, mount the well platform and begin turning the drill. As it probes untested ground, offering new and exciting discoveries, let it sink deeper and deeper. Eventually, you will tap into the rich reserve of ministry gifts God has formed just for you.

The stark gymnasium echoes with every bump and clatter as the fifty boys at the juvenile hall slowly file into their seats for Sunday chapel. One man from a local church leads a few songs, another speaks briefly, and finally, Phil stands up to give his testimony. He nervously stutters and shakes through his two-minute speech and then sits down . . . discouraged.

But after the service, Phil joins one small group of boys who have stayed to talk. Looking into their eyes, Phil's heart swells with compassion as they open up about their lives. He wants to hug each love-starved one and tell him about Jesus. The counseling time ends too soon for Phil. It is his first experience showing mercy to others, and he longs to come back to see them next Sunday. Phil is tapping into his spiritual gift.

Initially, Phil thought he had failed in his ministry with the juvenile hall boys. But speaking may not have been his spiritual gift. Have you ever attempted using a spiritual gift and felt as discouraged as Phil? Describe the situation, and from the chart in our lesson, try to pinpoint the gift you may have tried using.

_____

_____

_____

_____

Like drilling and coming up dry, sometimes we try a certain ministry and sense no effectiveness or ease. But at other times, as when Phil began showing mercy to the boys, God uses us in powerful ways. And we want to give of ourselves again and again.

Have you ministered in a way that has been effective and easy? Describe those circumstances, and from the chart, take a guess at the gift or gifts you might have been using.

_____

_____

_____

_____

If you have never really experienced joy in ministry, if the effectiveness and ease we have talked about is unfamiliar to you, don't be discouraged. Through the next nine lessons in this study, we will be exploring the gifts in detail, and you will be given opportunities to discover which one is yours. For now, know that God has gifted you, and keep ministering in different ways—before you know it, you'll be experiencing the thrill of ministry too.

 Living Insights ────────────────────────── STUDY TWO

Through the spiritual gifts, Christians relate to one another in a perfectly balanced, God-designed system. Each believer serves a specific need in the church. This means that you and the gift you possess are vital. Without you, the church is like a three-wheeled car—bumping and scraping along.

Read Ephesians 4:15–16. What does Paul say the church requires in order to function well?

_____

_____

What do you think would happen if certain parts of the church body were absent or nonfunctioning (see vv. 11–14)?

_____

_____

How does it make you feel to know that you are so needed for the church to relate well and grow?

_____

_____

When you attend your church this Sunday, start looking for signs of a three-wheeled car. Find ways in which you can make your church run more smoothly. You just may be the part that's missing.

Chapter 2

GIFTS THAT GRAB OUR ATTENTION

1 Corinthians 12:14–27; Ephesians 4:11–13

Think how you would feel if this happened to you . . .

You have a friend who lives in a city many, many miles away; and because of this great distance, you haven't been able to see each other for years. Every Christmas, though, you try to make up for that distance by taking great care and effort in choosing just the right gift. Even the details of the wrapping reflect your love and respect for your friend, as you select elegant paper and colorful, exquisite bows.

Then one day, out of the blue, someone sends you enough money to make a long-dreamed-of visit to your friend. Bubbling with anticipation, you travel the many miles, finally reveling in your friend's warm welcome. Talking and laughing like two giddy kids, you share a wonderful ride from the airport, until at last you've arrived at your friend's home. After a few moments, you pause to survey the living room, but see none of your gifts on display. While still chatting, you glance into the den, the kitchen, the hallway— no gifts. Your heart begins to sink, but you don't have the courage to ask about the gifts.

While your friend is away on an errand, however, you peek into the front closet, and your heart drops. There, after all these years, are all the once-glittering gifts you sent, still wrapped and unused. How would you feel?

As you think through your own emotions, perhaps you can imagine a little of how God feels. For He has sent us beautifully wrapped and carefully selected gifts as tender expressions of His love for us (James 1:17), yet many of us have stored these gifts in a closet—unopened, unused. As a result, we may be missing the special way in which God wants to use us through our gifts.

A Brief Review of the Gifts

In order to know more about God's treasures for us, let's take a moment to review the basic facts about spiritual gifts.

What They Are

In the last lesson, we discovered that there are a variety of gifts used in many types of ministries, resulting in a multitude of benefits for the body of Christ (1 Cor. 12:4–7). We also learned the definition of spiritual gifts: *They are abilities or skills given to each Christian, enabling us to function in particular capacities with ease and effectiveness for the glory of God.* These gifts are listed for us in Romans 12, 1 Corinthians 12, Ephesians 4, and 1 Peter 4.

One characteristic of the gifts in these lists is that, like prisms, they flash a broad spectrum of abilities and skills. Music, counseling, and the ability to learn languages may reflect the various hues of certain gifts, while other gifts may radiate abilities such as hospitality, problem solving, craftsmanship, or even celibacy. As a result, God's multifaceted spiritual gifts can be expressed by each of us in different ways.

Why They Are Important

These gifts have value not only because they come from the hand of our Lord, but also because, like a springtime rain, they shower us as a body of believers with inestimable benefits.

First, *they keep the body balanced.* Most of us like to pursue our one favorite interest, treading the same path until we've worn it into a rut. But the variety of spiritual gifts keeps the body of Christ moving in many directions, safeguarding us against extremes or preoccupations.

Second, *they keep the church healthy.* Since every believer has a spiritual gift, the burden of ministry can be shared equally. Often, ministries collapse from exhaustion when too few people are doing too many jobs. However, when gift-exercising Christians help shoulder the weight, the church blossoms with a healthy vitality.

Third, *they keep the focus clear.* When spiritual gifts are all working together, our eyes are irresistibly drawn to the Giver, and we can't help but glorify Him from the joyful overflow of our hearts.

The apostle Paul illustrates each of these three points in a memorable analogy that also reveals his sense of humor.

> For the body is not one member, but many. If the foot should say, "Because I am not a hand, I am not a part of the body," it is not for this reason any the less a part of the body. And if the ear should say, "Because I am not an eye, I am not a part of the

body," it is not for this reason any the less a part of the body. If the whole body were an eye, where would the hearing be? If the whole were hearing, where would the sense of smell be? But now God has placed the members, each one of them, in the body, just as He desired. And if they were all one member, where would the body be? But now there are many members, but one body. And the eye cannot say to the hand, "I have no need of you"; or again the head to the feet, "I have no need of you." On the contrary, it is much truer that the members of the body which seem to be weaker are necessary. (1 Cor. 12:14–22)

With his absurd cast of talking eyes and six-foot-tall ears, the Apostle makes his point: *everybody* is needed. Even the seemingly smallest gift is necessary for the whole body to function properly.

And since we are all parts of one body, we would gain immensely from learning how we all interrelate. Like medical students, we need to learn all we can about anatomy—only in our case, the anatomy of Christ's spiritual body, the church. And as most anatomy classes begin, we must start by categorizing the parts.

A Simple Way to Categorize the Gifts

Ways to categorize the gifts of the Spirit abound, but one helpful way is a threefold division that considers the gifts' functions.

Support Gifts

The support gifts are foundational. Like the heart and lungs, they are vital to the body of Christ because they provide direction and leadership for the church.

Service Gifts

The service gifts work behind the scenes, quietly encouraging and building up the body.

Sign Gifts

Finally, the sign gifts supernaturally manifest the Holy Spirit's power, authenticating God's presence in the church. These gifts could never be mistaken for someone's natural abilities.

The following chart lists the gifts in each of these categories.[1]

Support Gifts	Service Gifts	Sign Gifts
Apostleship/Word of wisdom Prophecy/Word of knowledge Evangelism Pastor-Teacher Teaching	Administration/ Leading Exhortation Faith Giving Helps/Serving Showing mercy	Distinguishing of spirits Miracles Healings Tongues Interpretation of tongues

A General Understanding of the Support Gifts

Let's further our anatomical analysis of the body of Christ by examining more closely the first category of gifts, the support gifts.

Apostleship

The first gift that we will consider in the support category is apostleship (see 1 Cor. 12:28). This gift was bestowed upon certain men, called apostles,[2] who had absolute authority as spiritual leaders in the early church (see Acts 6:2–4). Endued with great wisdom, they devoted themselves to founding churches, writing Scripture, and forging out the tenets of the faith (see Eph. 2:19–21). Perhaps their wisdom resulted from the gift "word of wisdom," which closely parallels the gift of apostleship.[3]

In addition to leading and teaching, apostles performed miraculous signs and wonders that authenticated their role in the early church (see Acts 3:1–7; 20:7–12). Apostleship also has the distinction of being bestowed only on those who had seen the risen Christ, which included Paul (see 1 Cor. 9:1).

Does this gift exist today? Nowhere does the Scripture indicate that apostolic authority passed beyond the few who had it in the

1. The gifts listed in the chart are those specifically mentioned in Scripture as spiritual gifts. Possibly, however, there are other spiritual gifts that are not designated as clearly, but nevertheless function in the church. Such possible gifts include hospitality, music, craftsmanship, counseling, celibacy, and others.

2. The word *apostle* comes from the Greek word *apostolos*, meaning "sent one." From its Latin equivalent we derive our word *missionary*.

3. In the listings of spiritual gifts in 1 Corinthians 12, "apostles" and "prophets" head two of the lists (v. 28 and vv. 29–30), while "word of wisdom" and "word of knowledge" head one (vv. 8–10). Possibly then, the gift word of wisdom is related to apostleship, and word of knowledge to prophecy. See William McRae's *Dynamics of Spiritual Gifts* (Grand Rapids, Mich.: Zondervan Publishing House, 1976), pp. 64–66.

New Testament. So in seeking to discover our gift, we need not consider apostleship as an option; nor should we give credence to those who claim to be modern apostles.

Prophecy

Following apostleship is the gift of prophecy (1 Cor. 12:28). The two differ in that apostles were *sent forth*, while prophets *spoke forth*. Apostles had the gift of word of wisdom, while prophets had the gift of word of knowledge.[4] Prophets were inspired to communicate God's Word for the present—"forthtelling"; and for the future—foretelling. And most significantly, they always spoke without error (see Deut. 18:21–22).

This amazing spiritual gift was highly valued, because the New Testament had not been completed and the early church needed to know God's Word. So as a result of their insights, revelations, and visions, the prophets warned, reproved, and encouraged the people. Paul summed it up when he wrote, "One who prophesies edifies the church" (1 Cor. 14:4b).

Sometimes today we rightly say that a teacher who has deep insight into Scripture and who can wisely evaluate our times is a "prophet." The spiritual gift of prophecy, however, was limited to those who voiced God's revelation, a practice no longer necessary since we have the completed Bible.

Evangelism

In Ephesians 4:11, evangelism is listed as the next gift after apostleship and prophecy. Evangelists are "gospelizers"; they communicate the good news, or gospel, of Jesus Christ to the lost. Coupled with their God-given zeal for the unsaved is an inspired creativity and clarity in explaining the gospel. They can put the cookies on the bottom shelf, so to speak, and people usually respond to them amicably.

Evangelists come from all corners of God's house: some lead large public crusades and some work one-on-one; some love to share the gospel with youth and some yearn to spread the word to internationals. Whatever the emphasis, the spiritually gifted evangelist always warms people to Jesus.

---

4. The two gifts, prophecy and word of knowledge, were probably in action together when Peter supernaturally knew about Ananias and Sapphira's secret withholding of money from the church (Acts 5:1–5).

Pastor-Teacher

While the evangelist goes where the lost are, the pastor-teacher[5] stays in one locale and shepherds those already in God's fold. Along with their shepherding gift, pastor-teachers comfort, encourage, and guard others while at the same time instructing, reproving, and equipping them. In fact, if you would like to read their job description, take a look at 1 Timothy 3:1–7; 2 Timothy 4:1–5; and 1 Peter 5:1–4.

Along with these requirements are four checkpoints anyone with this gift must pass. First, pastor-teachers need to be *faithful*, staying committed to the flock in good times and bad. Second, pastor-teachers need to be *practical*, not afraid to address the problems of daily life. Third, they need to be *discerning*, able to spot danger before it's obvious, distinguish the phony from the real, and sense the struggles of the flock. Finally, they need to be *able to take criticism*, for people have a tendency to throw darts at their leaders, and pastor-teachers must have thick skins to protect themselves emotionally.

A Personal Response to Those with These Gifts

Let's pause here and reflect on the spiritual gifts we have unwrapped so far—apostleship, prophecy, evangelism, and pastor-teacher. Where would Christianity be if these gifts had remained in the closet, unopened and unused? There would be no church, no New Testament, no worldwide spread of the gospel, and no shepherdlike protection from the world's ravenous wolves.

Surely these gifts are priceless treasures that God has given to the church. As we specifically consider the two that remain in effect today—evangelism and pastor-teacher—let's apply a couple of crucial principles.

First, to those who possess these support gifts, *be an example of what you proclaim*. As Paul wrote to pastor Timothy, "In speech, conduct, love, faith and purity, show yourself an example of those who believe" (1 Tim. 4:12b).

---

5. In Ephesians 4:11, the phrase reads, "And He gave some as . . . pastors and teachers." Referring to the word *and*, one Greek scholar wrote, "Often the word has the meaning 'that is' or 'in particular' and indicates that the 'shepherds' and 'teachers' are viewed as one common group, i.e., 'teaching shepherds.'" Fritz Rienecker, *A Linguistic Key to the Greek New Testament*, ed. Cleon L. Rogers, Jr. (Grand Rapids, Mich.: Zondervan Publishing House, Regency Reference Library, 1980), p. 531.

Second, to those who receive the benefits from men and women with support gifts, *hold these people in high regard* (see 1 Tim. 5:17–18; Heb. 13:7, 17). Respect them as gifts from God. Encourage them. Meet their needs.

Do you think you might have the gift of evangelism? The gift of pastor-teacher? Possibly some other gift? Keep unwrapping until you find out. But don't leave your gift in the closet—it's far too valuable to hide.

 ## *Living Insights* STUDY ONE

What comes to mind when you hear the word *evangelist?* Do you automatically think of the media's often-insulting caricatures of smooth-talking, teeth-flashing, hand-in-your-wallet salesmen?

God's true evangelists, though, are anything but money-hungry con artists. They are usually ordinary folks who just want to help others find heaven. Could you have the gift of evangelism? The following questions may help you decide.

Do you find yourself in situations in which the topics of Christ and salvation come up?

☐ Often   ☐ Sometimes   ☐ Rarely

Do you gravitate toward relationships with non-Christians?

☐ Often   ☐ Sometimes   ☐ Rarely

When you explain the gospel to others, do they clearly understand it?

☐ Often   ☐ Sometimes   ☐ Rarely

When others hear you explain the gospel, do they respond by trusting Christ?

☐ Often   ☐ Sometimes   ☐ Rarely

Let these questions stimulate your thinking. The Lord will show you if you have the gift of evangelism. And even if you don't, share the gospel freely—it's the best gift anyone can give.

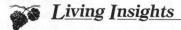 *Living Insights* STUDY TWO

In *Feeding and Leading*, Dr. Ken Gangel lists the top reasons why volunteers in the church quit their ministries.

- Because willing people become overworked and burned out.

- Because volunteers don't receive much-needed help.

- Because lay people have personal and spiritual needs of their own which aren't being met in the framework of their ministries.

- Because we do not adequately show apprecia- tion. . . .

- Because friction has developed between or among workers in a given ministry area.[6]

Those who faithfully minister in the church, who teach our children and care for our families, are a valuable resource in our churches. But, as you can see from Dr. Gangel's list, those with support gifts often work so hard to meet our needs that inside they dry up, burn out, and shrivel away. And we may never know about it until they hand in their resignation.

If the body of Christ were functioning as it should, how could these causes for dropping out be avoided (see 1 Cor. 12:14–27)?

_____

_____

_____

Do you know people in your church with a support gift? How can you encourage them? What practical way can you think of to give them a hand in their ministry?

_____

_____

6. Kenneth O. Gangel, *Feeding and Leading* (Wheaton, Ill.: Scripture Press Publications, Victor Books, 1989), p. 146.

_____

_____

_____

Maybe you are the one with the support gift who feels close to quitting. One of Dr. Gangel's reasons for dropping out may particularly apply to your situation. If that is the case, which reason is it?

_____

_____

Knowing why you feel discouraged in your ministry is the first step. Now think of what you can do to turn that cause for quitting around. Write down some of your ideas.

_____

_____

_____

The apostle Paul wrote,

> There should be no division in the body, but . . . the members should have the same care for one another. And if one member suffers, all the members suffer with it; if one member is honored, all the members rejoice with it." (1 Cor. 12:25–26)

Let those words be your motto as you care for one another in your church.

Chapter 3

THE PASTOR-TEACHER, THE TEACHER ... AND THE TAUGHT

Selected Scripture

We donned our hard hats in the last lesson and began an on-site survey of the foundational or support gifts. These abilities, according to Ephesians 4:12, are "for the equipping of the saints . . . the building up of the body of Christ." To better visualize how this "building up" works, let's take a moment to examine the following blueprint:

Gifts That Support the Body of Christ
Ephesians 4:11–12

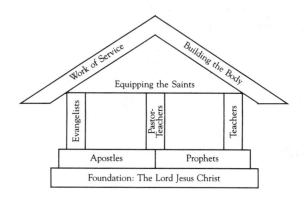

As the diagram illustrates, Christ our Savior is the cornerstone, the apostles and prophets are built upon Him, and the evangelists, pastor-teachers, and teachers form the sturdy pillars that uphold the rest of the structure. In our previous study, we only got about half-way through the middle column and hadn't yet examined the third. So now let's put our hard hats back on and finish our architectural exploration.

A Quick Review: Three Support Gifts

We need to make sure that the cement of our understanding is dry before we proceed with our inspection of the last two support gifts. A quick review, then, is in order.

The first group we considered were the *significant leaders of the early church: the apostles.* These men established the foundational creeds and doctrines of our faith and recorded the living words of our living God in the New Testament. Gifted with miraculous powers and great courage, they also founded churches all over the world. Once these purposes had been accomplished, though, there was no longer any need for this absolute apostolic authority. So this gift is no longer present in the church today.

Next we looked at the *inerrant messengers of the early church: the prophets.* Through revelations and visions, prophets received the divine message and then spoke it forth without error. Their role in communicating God's Word was essential because the New Testament had not yet been completed. Since we now have the Scriptures in their fullness, however, this gift has also passed on and is not available for today's church.

Finally, we met the *itinerant witnesses to the unsaved world: the evangelists.* These specially endowed people bring the light of Christ's good news to darkened souls, making grace and truth easy to reach. Still vital and vibrant, this gift will be a part of the church until Christ returns.

With these three gifts set firmly in our minds, let's now do a little surveying work on the other two.

A Further Look: Two More Support Gifts

The two gifts we have left to study, pastor-teacher and teacher, sound almost identical. However, despite their similarities, these roles have some important differences—differences that are crucial in discerning whether we have the gift and pivotal in our expectations for those who do. Because we started our study of the pastor-teacher gift in our last lesson, we'll pick it up first here.

The Role of the Pastor-Teacher

The most accurate picture of the role of a pastor-teacher is the shepherd. Unlike evangelists who come, preach the gospel to the unsaved, and leave, pastor-teachers shepherd God's flock—guarding, comforting, and instructing long-term. Those with this gift may be seminary-trained or self-taught, full-time professionals or part-time volunteers; but three characteristics always remain true.

First, the gift of pastor-teacher *involves a calling from God.* Ephesians 4:11 specifically says, *"He gave* some as . . . pastors and teachers" (emphasis added). This calling is a divine motivation that comes in a variety of ways—dramatically and suddenly for some people, quietly and steadily for others. But if it is real, it will produce an inner thirst that no other occupation will satisfy.

Second, the gift of pastor-teacher *includes the strictest of standards.* For example, the character qualifications are uncompromising:

> It is a trustworthy statement: if any man aspires to the office of overseer, it is a fine work he desires to do. An overseer, then, must be above reproach, the husband of one wife, temperate, prudent, respectable, hospitable, able to teach, not addicted to wine or pugnacious, but gentle, uncontentious, free from the love of money. He must be one who manages his own household well, keeping his children under control with all dignity (but if a man does not know how to manage his own household, how will he take care of the church of God?); and not a new convert, lest he become conceited and fall into the condemnation incurred by the devil. And he must have a good reputation with those outside the church, so that he may not fall into reproach and the snare of the devil. (1 Tim. 3:1–7)

And the tasks are rigorous.

> Preach the word; be ready in season and out of season; reprove, rebuke, exhort, with great patience and instruction. For the time will come when they will not endure sound doctrine; but wanting to have their ears tickled, they will accumulate for themselves teachers in accordance to their own desires; and will turn away their ears from the truth, and will turn aside to myths. But you, be sober in all things, endure hardship, do the work of an evangelist, fulfill your ministry. (2 Tim. 4:2–5)

In addition, the pastor-teacher's attitudes are to be noble and pure.

Therefore, I exhort the elders among you, as your fellow elder and witness of the sufferings of Christ, and a partaker also of the glory that is to be revealed, shepherd the flock of God among you, exercising oversight not under compulsion, but voluntarily, according to the will of God; and not for sordid gain, but with eagerness; nor yet as lording it over those allotted to your charge, but proving to be examples to the flock. And when the Chief Shepherd appears, you will receive the unfading crown of glory. You younger men, likewise, be subject to your elders; and all of you, clothe yourselves with humility toward one another, for God is opposed to the proud, but gives grace to the humble. (1 Pet. 5:1–5)

According to these instructions, those with this spiritual gift must serve God's people willingly, eagerly, and humbly—lofty attitudes indeed. But the highest attitude of all is that the pastor-teacher must have a fierce and insatiable love for God. In their book *Liberating Ministry from the Success Syndrome*, Kent and Barbara Hughes write:

> *Before all things, even service to God, we must love God with all of our hearts.* It is the highest priority in life! . . .
> Everything we have is to be devoted to our loving God. This theme was substantiated and solemnized by the Lord himself when a lawyer asked him, "Teacher, which is the greatest commandment in the Law?" To which Jesus answered, "You shall love the Lord your God with all your heart and with all your soul and with all your mind. This is the first and greatest commandment" (Matthew 22:37–38). From Jesus' own lips we hear that nothing, nothing is of greater importance![1]

The third characteristic of the pastor-teacher gift is that it *implies modeling and mentoring.* Peter commanded the leaders of the church to shepherd by "proving to be examples to the flock" (1 Pet. 5:3);

---

1. Kent and Barbara Hughes, *Liberating Ministry from the Success Syndrome* (Wheaton, Ill.: Tyndale House Publishers, 1987), p. 58.

he knew the worth of living what one claims to believe. And he also knew the value of mentoring, of investing oneself in others' lives to impact the church in the future. As a result of this modeling and mentoring, people are changed and the torch of truth passes from generation to generation.

The pastor-teacher pillar certainly bears much weight as it supports the church, but there is one more indispensable column: the teacher.

The Gift of Being a Teacher

In 1 Peter 4:10–11, the apostle Peter refers to the gift of teaching as speaking. Whether we call it speaking or teaching, two points become clear about this gift.

First, *the meaning of the gift is "to give instruction."* Spiritually gifted teachers are able to communicate the truth of God accurately, clearly, and simply. Unlike the prophet, who voiced original revelation directly from God, the teacher explains what has already been revealed. And unlike the pastor-teacher, the teacher isn't necessarily a shepherd. Instead, the teacher's main goal is to empower the church with spiritual muscle by declaring the truth and inspiring Christians to stand up to false teachers (see Acts 20:18b–21).

Second, *the exercising of the gift requires four loves.* Like the pastor-teacher, those with the gift of teaching have a divine thirst within them that expresses itself in the following ways:

(1) *They love the body.* They understand the dangers of biblical ignorance and truly care about Christians being well-equipped with the truth.
(2) *They love studying the Bible.* They consider digging truths out of Scripture a treasure-hunting adventure, a true joy.
(3) *They love delivering the truth.* Finding the golden nuggets of truth is only the beginning, for teachers have a passion for revealing what they've found to others.
(4) *They love simplicity.* With a talent for simplifying the complicated, they know how to illustrate their points and keep their ideas interesting. As a result, they are able to widen the eyes of their students and make the truth come alive.

Two irreplaceable pillars of the church: pastor-teacher and teacher. They sound so similar, though. Is there really much difference between them?

A Few Interesting Comparisons

The following chart helps clarify the fine distinctions between the two.

Pastor-Teacher	Teacher
The pastor needs to have the gift of teaching.	The teacher does not need the gift of shepherding.
Leadership skills are essential to the pastor.	To the teacher managerial skills are optional.
The church is the best setting for the pastor's work.	The teacher can exercise this gift in a variety of locations.

Some Practical Suggestions: To All Who Are Taught

Only a few of us will have one of these two gifts, but we all benefit from them. So let's turn our attention to our responsibilities as "the taught."

Be supportive. Paul writes specifically to those who receive instruction,

> And let the one who is taught the word share
> all good things with him who teaches. (Gal. 6:6)

What does "all good things" mean? Simply this: we should affirm, encourage, and pray for our leaders. Such positive affirmation builds strong braces that will strengthen them even when winds of criticism blow.

Be generous. Not only should we support our pastors and teachers with encouraging words, but we should also take care of their material needs.

> Let the elders who rule well be considered worthy
> of double honor, especially those who work hard at
> preaching and teaching. For the Scripture says, "You
> shall not muzzle the ox while he is threshing," and
> "The laborer is worthy of his wages." (1 Tim. 5:17–18)

Those who "labor" become exhausted when, like muzzled oxen, they are deprived of nourishment. Learners can strengthen their pastors and teachers by offering them needed money, time, or even a helping hand. All these gifts bolster them for the long haul.

Be teachable. Nothing motivates pastors or teachers more than when those entrusted to their care begin to flower. This growth only results when students are attentive and responsive, ready and eager to learn. These kinds of learners are a leader's greatest source of joy.

> Remember those who led you, who spoke the word of God to you; and considering the result of their conduct, imitate their faith. . . . Obey your leaders, and submit to them; for they keep watch over your souls, as those who will give an account. Let them do this with joy and not with grief, for this would be unprofitable for you. (Heb. 13:7, 17)

A Concluding Thought

Those who possess the support gifts and faithfully minister to us are God's gardeners, cultivating and pruning us. They are the church's pillars, shoring us up and giving us strength. And they are the voices God uses to call us to Himself. So to those who love us and teach us, let's not forget to say, "Thanks!"

 Living Insights STUDY ONE

Ever watch how people get into a swimming pool? Some people head straight for the diving board, and without so much as a wince, they bounce, bounce, and plunge into the water. Others only feel brave enough to go in one step at a time. Then half an hour of temperature adjustments later, they finally shove off into the water like christened luxury liners. The last group never actually make it into the pool. Putting one toe in the water convinces them they'll just watch today, thank you.

In a similar way, some people know they have the gift of pastor-teacher or teacher, and they dive right in. Others know pastoring or teaching is not for them. Maybe, though, you think you might have one of these gifts, but you're timid and unsure. Your answers to the following questions may reveal whether you have these gifts.

Perhaps you have the gift of *pastoring*. Do you feel God's calling to pastor?[2] Explain how.

_____

_____

---

2. Receiving God's call to be a pastor does not necessarily mean you have to fill the office of pastor. Many exercise their pastoral gift as lay people in the church.

Do you meet the qualifications for the gift of pastor-teacher outlined in the lesson (1 Tim. 3:1–7; 2 Tim. 4:2–5; 1 Pet. 5:1–5)?

Do you feel a yearning to model the principles of Scripture and mentor others so that they can follow Christ also? Describe your inner desire.

If you think you might have the gift of *teaching*, go through the following checklist based on the four loves discussed in the lesson.

☐ I love the body of Christ and desire that others know more about Scripture.

☐ I love studying the Word of God.

☐ I love communicating the principles I learn from the Bible.

☐ I love making complicated truths simple and understandable.

Should you discover that the Lord has gifted you as a pastor or teacher, learn more about your gift.[3] It's not enough to know your gift; you must develop it too. And when you're ready, begin expressing it right away. Go ahead, dive in!

3. The following resources will further your understanding of these two gifts: Lawrence O. Richards, *Creative Bible Teaching* (Chicago, Ill.: Moody Press, 1970); Howard G. Hendricks, *Teaching to Change Lives* (Portland, Oreg.: Multnomah Press; Atlanta, Ga.: Walk Thru the Bible Ministries, 1987); Eugene H. Peterson, *Five Smooth Stones for Pastoral Work* (Atlanta, Ga.: John Knox Press, 1980); and two by John R. W. Stott, *Between Two Worlds* (Grand Rapids, Mich.: William B. Eerdmans Publishing Co., 1982) and *The Preacher's Portrait* (Grand Rapids, Mich.: William B. Eerdmans Publishing Co., 1984).

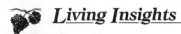

Who was your spiritual teacher? Who was the one whose eyes sparkled when you answered correctly, whose hand guarded you from the foolishness of youth, and whose heartbeat embraced your soul when you yearned for something to believe in?

Write down the name of this person from your past who so impacted your life.

_____

Perhaps you have a pastor, Sunday school teacher, or friend who is impacting you now. What is this individual's name?

_____

As you consider these and other pastors and teachers in your life, are you supportive of them? How could you encourage them this week?

_____

_____

_____

Are you generous in meeting their needs? Write down tangible ways to help them and show how much you love them.

_____

_____

_____

Are you teachable when they are sharing God's principles with you? How could you respond better to their teaching?

_____

_____

_____

Chapter 4

A SALUTE TO THE SERVERS

Romans 12:1–7; 1 Corinthians 12:28

Crinkle, crinkle. The noise was almost imperceptible above the din of the airport lobby, but the woman definitely heard it. Waiting for her flight, she had purchased a newspaper and a package of cookies and sat down to enjoy both . . . crinkle, crinkle. She heard it again! She couldn't see what it was because she had opened the newspaper in front of her. But she could hear it, and her first thought was "My cookies."

Peeking over a corner of the paper, she saw a tie-and-briefcase man across the tiny table from her, helping himself to her cookies. Not knowing what else to do, she slid the treats to her side of the table, slipped out a cookie to show ownership, and retreated behind the newspaper. End of encounter.

On page three, she heard it again. Crinkle, crinkle, crunch. She glanced over—the man was still chewing the evidence. "Who does this guy think he is!" she fumed inside. Reaching over to reclaim her treasure, she saw him move. For an instant, they locked eyes, then together looked down at the package. The last, lonely cookie stared back. Pausing for a moment, the man finally took the cookie and, with a frown, broke it, pushing the other half across the table. As he left to catch his flight, she took the morsel and retreated again to her paper, dumbfounded by his audacity.

When her flight was announced, she gladly moved to the gate, still shaking her head about the cookies. Seeing the attendant's outstretched hand, though, snapped her back to the present. "Oh yes, my ticket," she said. Opening her purse, she found the ticket, but that was not all. Perched on top was her *uneaten* package of cookies! She spun around to look for the man, but all that remained was his wadded-up cookie package and a few crumbs.

Isn't it amazing how wrong some assumptions can be? What we take for granted as true can sometimes be just the opposite of truth. Often, as in our cookie story, wrong assumptions are quite harmless. But at other times, as with spiritual gifts, they can be very costly.

Popular Assumptions, Erroneously Believed

Most Christians make three wrong assumptions about spiritual gifts—assumptions that could effectually cripple the body of Christ.

"Only the Visible Are Vital"

Although people may not say it directly, their words imply the misconception that only the visible are vital: "I'm just an usher; the pastor is the one who can tell you all about our church. . . . I think I'll take John to the crusade tonight; I'm sure that evangelist can lead him to Christ much better than I. . . . I'm sure God would rather hear that beautiful choir than me trying to make my 'joyful noise'!" All these statements suggest that the one with the more visible gift is more capable and therefore more important.

But think about that for a moment. We are the *body* of Christ, functioning much like the human body (1 Cor. 12), and we'd never make this assumption about ourselves, now would we? Just think of what a doctor examines first at a checkup—not what is visible, like whether our head is still on straight or whether our face is still the same. He checks our vital signs—pulse, temperature, blood pressure—all things we cannot see (compare vv. 21–25 especially).

"Only the Public Gifts Will Be Rewarded"

Another erroneous assumption is that only people with public gifts will get rewards. After all, they are in leadership and work at ministry day in, day out. But we only need to take a quick look at Scripture to be reassured that those who serve unnoticed will be rewarded too.

> For God is not unjust so as to forget your work and the love which you have shown toward His name, in having ministered and in still ministering to the saints. (Heb. 6:10; see also 2 Tim. 1:16–18, where Paul's friend Onesiphorous receives special honor)

Through God's one-way mirror, He sees our hidden ministries. And being a just Lord, He will remember to reward us for any and every task done in His name. Paul pointed this out when comparing his own work to the ministry of Apollos:

> I planted, Apollos watered, but God was causing the growth. So then neither the one who plants nor the one who waters is anything, but God who causes the growth. Now he who plants and he who waters are one; but *each will receive his own reward according to his own labor.* (1 Cor. 3:6–8, emphasis added)

Paul was not favored over Apollos; and neither is someone else over you. God weighs each of us in relation to our own gift.

"Only the Head of the Body Is Important"

A third false assumption rings so close to true that some people would be shocked to consider it false. Since Christ is the head of the body of believers (Eph. 4:15; 5:23; Col. 1:18), some may assume that *only* the head is important. But Paul makes the implication of that statement clear:

> The eye cannot say to the hand, "I have no need of you"; or again the head to the feet, "I have no need of you." (1 Cor. 12:21)

Certainly Christ alone is the head, but He alone does not perform all the functions of the body. We do that, by following His strategy, carrying out His directions, and relying on His power. So even though you may sometimes feel unworthy, you really are valuable to God—so valuable that Christ died to redeem you. And that redemption is for a purpose, so that you can play a vital role in His eternal drama.

Because you play such an important part, you must know what your role is and be prepared to enact it. It is essential, then, to listen closely to Christ, the Director, who has some crucial instructions for you.

General Instructions, Easily Forgotten

In his epistle to the Romans, Paul hands us these instructions—directives that address how we relate to God, ourselves, and others.

Regarding Our Relationship with God

> I urge you therefore, brethren, by the mercies of God, to present your bodies a living and holy sacrifice, acceptable to God, which is your spiritual service of worship. And do not be conformed to this world, but be transformed by the renewing of your mind, that you may prove what the will of God is, that which is good and acceptable and perfect. (Rom. 12:1–2)

The first step in relating to God is to *present ourselves to Him.* In sacrificing our selfish desires, we commit ourselves to obeying

29

God alone. Consequently, we become available to Him so that He can accomplish His purposes through our gifts.

The other side of this command is important as well: *protect yourself from the world.* By saying, "Do not be conformed to this world" (v. 2), Paul means that we should not let the world shape our values and character so that we are indistinguishable from non-Christians. For if we allow ourselves to be squeezed into the world's mold instead of sculpted by God's will, our gifts become blunted and the artwork of our lives is desecrated.

In the next verse, the subject turns to how we should view ourselves.

Regarding Our Assessment of Ourselves

> For through the grace given to me I say to every man among you not to think more highly of himself than he ought to think; but to think so as to have sound judgment, as God has allotted to each a measure of faith. (v. 3)

In playing our part in the body of Christ, we need to watch our tendency to upstage others, to be conceited and arrogant. Yet we should avoid the opposite pitfall as well, because assessing ourselves as worthless and unimportant is just as wrong. Rather, we should "have sound judgment" concerning ourselves and our gifts, realizing others' uniqueness and our own.

Having prepared us to handle our giftedness with a proper attitude toward God and self, Paul next gives us instructions concerning how our gifts help us relate to others.

Regarding Our Contribution to Others

> For just as we have many members in one body and all the members do not have the same function, so we, who are many, are one body in Christ, and individually members one of another. And since we have gifts that differ according to the grace given to us, let each exercise them accordingly. (vv. 4–6a)

Through God's grace, we are far more than mere links in a chain —each just like the next, all appearing as cold, lifeless, machine-stamped nonentities. Instead, we are living, vibrant persons, interconnected and interdependent members of Christ's body, yet uniquely gifted for particular functions and ministries.

Specific Directions, Carefully Stated

Christ's instructions concerning our part in His drama become more specific as Paul identifies some of the spiritual gifts in verses 6b–8.[1] He lists two support gifts, prophecy and teaching (vv. 6b, 7b), but emphasizes the service gifts by including five of them: serving, exhorting, giving, administrating, and showing mercy (vv. 7–8).[2] For the balance of our lesson, we'll focus on the first of the service gifts, *serving*—which we'll combine with *helps*, a gift Paul mentions in 1 Corinthians 12:28.[3] The serving/helping gift is *the ability to assist and support others in practical and behind-the-scenes ways that cause public ministries to run smoothly and effortlessly.*

Like the inner workings of an ornate hall clock, those with this gift tirelessly tick away in the background, ensuring the effectiveness of the dials and hands. From the outside we may not see servers; but like clocks without cogs and flywheels, ministries without these gifted people would simply stop.

Effective ministries, however, are always equipped with willing servers and helpers who take delight in their duties. Hard workers and self-starters, they also have insight to see needs and meet them, often without being told, in their quiet and humble way. And they would much rather do their work unnoticed because, frankly, the limelight makes them nervous.

Such faithful servers fill the New Testament, but, characteristically, you have to look hard to find them. A few examples are Epaphroditus, Dorcas, and Onesimus (Phil. 2:25; Acts 9:36; Philem. 10–11). Paul briefly highlights one other woman with this gift in his letter to the Romans.

> I commend to you our sister Phoebe, who is a servant of the church which is at Cenchrea; that you

---

1. The categories of all the gifts are overviewed in chapter 2 of this study guide.

2. The sixth service gift, faith, is found in 1 Corinthians 12:9.

3. These two words, *serving* and *helps*, are very closely related in meaning. *Serving* comes from the Greek word *diakonia* and originally meant "wait on someone at table," later coming to mean "serve . . . care for . . . support." From a related word, *diakonos*, we derive our word *deacon*. The Greek word for *help*, *antilempsis*, literally means "a laying hold of," and the picture is of one person taking hold of another's weakness. In its plural form, it refers to the "ministrations of deacons." See Walter Bauer, *A Greek-English Lexicon of the New Testament*, trans. and ed. William F. Arndt, F. Wilbur Gingrich, and Frederick W. Danker, 2d ed., rev. and enl. (Chicago, Ill.: University of Chicago Press, 1979), p. 184; and G. Abbott-Smith, *A Manual Greek Lexicon of the New Testament*, 3d ed. (Edinburgh, Scotland: T. and T. Clark, 1937), p. 41.

receive her in the Lord in a manner worthy of the saints, and that you help her in whatever matter she may have need of you; for she herself has also been a helper of many, and of myself as well. (Rom. 16:1–2)

Phoebe was "a helper of many." In what ways did she help? Maybe she welcomed Paul into her home or made contacts for him in the city. We're not told, but Paul's highest respect went out to her.

In what ways do helpers serve the church today? They maintain the facilities, work in the kitchen, run the sound room, or cradle the little ones in the nursery. They draw the artwork, drive the elderly to services, print the bulletins, or arrange the flowers. And they do so much more, for they are what Paul called Phoebe—the servants of the church.[4]

Practical Conclusion, Personally Applied

Like Phoebe, those with gifts such as helping tend to slip into the back rows; however, two truths stand front and center as we reflect on their contributions to the church.

First, *harmony isn't in competition with individuality*. In the majestic harmonies of a full orchestra, we don't think of the musicians as competing with one another. The violinists aren't rivaling the cellists; neither is the lone oboist competing with the percussion section. Each member of the orchestra is unique, yet each blends with the other members in balanced harmony.

Second, *efficiency isn't nearly as important as creativity*. The church is not an impersonal machine—we are not called "God's robot" but His *body*. So efficiency should never bully creativity; God leaves room for the human element, and so should we.

In his book *Swim with the Sharks without Being Eaten Alive*, Harvey Mackay tells a story about an efficiency expert who went to hear a concert featuring Schubert's famous Unfinished Symphony. Afterward, the expert made these recommendations:

1. For considerable periods, the four oboe players had nothing to do. Their numbers should be reduced, and their work spread over the whole orchestra.

---

4. The Greek word translated *servant* is a form of *diakonos*. This passage, as well as 1 Timothy 3:11; 5:3–16 and 1 Corinthians 7:8, "may point to the earliest origins of the development of the later office of deaconess." J. Stam, "Deacon, Deaconess," in *The Zondervan Pictorial Encyclopedia of the Bible*, gen. ed. Merrill C. Tenney (Grand Rapids, Mich.: Zondervan Publishing House, Regency Reference Library, 1976), vol. 2, p. 49.

2. Forty violins were playing identical notes. This seems unnecessary duplication, and this section should be drastically cut. If a larger volume of sound is required, this could be achieved through an electronic amplifier.

3. Much effort was absorbed in the playing of demi/semi-quavers. This seems an excessive refinement, and it is recommended that all notes be rounded to the nearest semi-quaver. If this were done, it should be possible to use trainees and lower-grade operators.

4. No useful purpose is served by repeating with horns the passage that has already been handled by the strings. If all such redundant passages were eliminated, the concert could be reduced to twenty minutes. If Schubert had attended to these matters, he probably would have been able to finish his symphony after all.[5]

Of course, the efficiency expert's recommendations would destroy Schubert's masterpiece. Mackay makes his point: "Efficiency achieved at the expense of creativity is counterproductive."[6] As we learn about one another's gifts, we must remember that those who fill creative but quiet roles are just as important as the various components of a symphony—components that blend together to produce an enthralling work of art.

 ## Living Insights STUDY ONE

Do you think you might have the spiritual gift of serving/helping? To help you discern this, take the following test. Circle the answers that best describe you.

1. At church functions, like potlucks or camping trips, do you
   a. willingly volunteer to help with the details?
   b. have to be asked to help with the details?
   c. not think about the details?

5. Harvey B. Mackay, *Swim with the Sharks Without Being Eaten Alive* (New York, N.Y.: William Morrow and Company, Inc., 1988), pp. 157–58.

6. Mackay, *Swim with the Sharks*, p. 158.

2. Given the choice, would you rather
   a. set up the chairs or decorate for a church service?
   b. plan the order of worship for a church service?
   c. sing a solo at a church service?

3. If you were being honored at a church banquet, would you
   a. appreciate the honor, but be glad when it is over?
   b. greatly enjoy the attention?
   c. plan a ten-minute acceptance speech?

4. When others succeed as a result of your behind-the-scenes work, do you
   a. delight at their accomplishment?
   b. wish you could receive praise too?
   c. determine to be more up-front next time?

Obviously, if you circled *a* for each question, you may have the gift of serving/helping. But even for those who didn't circle the *a*'s, Christ's example of service is equally applicable.

> And calling them to Himself, Jesus said to them, "You know that those who are recognized as rulers of the Gentiles lord it over them; and their great men exercise authority over them. But it is not so among you, but whoever wishes to become great among you shall be your servant; and whoever wishes to be first among you shall be slave of all. For even the Son of Man did not come to be served, but to serve, and to give His life a ransom for many." (Mark 10:42–45)

Take time today to make yourself aware of the burdens of others. Even if you don't have the gift of serving/helping, you'll be standing side-by-side with the greatest servant of all—Jesus.

 Living Insights

Imagine a church newsletter that focused solely on the servers/helpers. What would some of the headlines be?

Greeters Doing a Great Job
Key Men Know How to Unlock Doors
George and Broom Sweep Up
Sound Room Hums on Sundays

Such headlines might make for a refreshing, although unusual, newsletter. Most of the time we give our attention to the more visible workers in the church, but those who serve faithfully behind the scenes deserve our appreciation too.

Can you think of some people in your church who serve and help unnoticed? What are their names?

_____

_____

Pick two or three of these people and brainstorm ways that you can show them your appreciation. Maybe your children can make a craft for them, or you can send them a note. Write down some of your ideas.

_____

_____

_____

Actually, the "Servants of the Church" newsletter might be a great idea! Give it some thought. But also think how much your church needs servers and helpers, and make sure to tell them thanks.

Chapter 5

GIFTS MOST MOTHERS MODEL
Selected Scripture

The little book *Love You Forever* portrays the lifelong love of a mother for her son. As a newborn, the son snuggles in his mother's arms while she sings him a tender song. As he grows, he grabs and splashes at age two, complains about baths at age nine, listens to screeching music as a teenager, and finally moves across town as a young man. But through these roller-coaster stages of life, his mother always takes a moment at night to sing her abiding love to him while he is sleeping. Her song is the same sweet lullaby that she sang to him as a baby:

> I'll love you forever,
> I'll like you for always,
> As long as I'm living,
> my baby you'll be.

The years pass. When she is old and sick, she calls her son to her and tries to sing the old, familiar song but is too weak to finish. So, cradling his mother in his arms, the son rocks her "back and forth, back and forth, back and forth" and sings her the song.

> I'll love you forever,
> I'll like you for always,
> As long as I'm living,
> my Mommy you'll be.

But the story is not over, for that night he returns to his home and gently picks up his baby daughter, rocking her and singing the same tender lullaby his mother sang over him.[1] Although his mother has died, her inexhaustible love crosses generations and lives forever in the song.

This enduring mother's love is a fitting illustration of the service gifts we will examine in today's lesson. For those who possess these

---

1. Robert Munsch, *Love You Forever* (Scarborough, Canada: Firefly Books, 1986).

gifts serve the church with a mother's faithfulness and love. A father may be the head of the family, but a mother is the heart, and those with the service gifts are just that . . . the heart of the church family. And just as ideal mothers faithfully serve the family, so those with the service gifts are to be faithful as well (see 1 Cor. 4:1–2).

Many more similarities exist between mothers and those with service gifts. The following analogies elaborate two of them.

Two Analogies Worth Considering

We can make two pertinent observations about mothers that help us more clearly define the role of those who serve the church.

First, *the mother's elevated title doesn't seem to fit her unsophisticated tasks.* Conferred on her at the birth of her firstborn, the title "mother" distinguishes a woman as an irreplaceable weaver of her child's character. Yet despite her influential position, her daily tasks are often common and mundane. For many mothers, sour diapers, endless cleaning, rainy-day carpooling, and tight-budget food-stretching fill the average day.

The world scoffs at these tasks, calling them unsophisticated. But such criticism will never tarnish a mother's lofty title and the crucial role she fills. Similarly, those with service gifts may never receive recognition by the congregation, but their function is nonetheless precious to the church and to Christ.

Second, *the mother's important responsibilities don't yield immediate results.* In fulfilling her role, a mother bears an armload of responsibilities. She shapes her children's character and models fairness, faithfulness, and consistency. She is unselfish, takes criticism, and enforces home rules. And she does all this, and much more, while trying to stay polite and positive!

But even though she gives and gives, the fruit of all that love and guidance is sometimes slow in coming. Years may pass before her children respond with "Thank you." Likewise, those who selflessly serve the church may work and work, receiving little in return. But the lack of immediate response from others is no indication of the value of their contribution.

Three Service Gifts Worth Emphasizing

In the previous lesson, we dug into one of these crucial service gifts, serving/helping. Now let's uncover three more service gifts—exhortation, giving, and administration—and see what we find.

The Gift of Exhorting

In the list of spiritual gifts in Romans 12:8, we discover the service gift of exhortation. *Exhortation* . . . sounds commanding, doesn't it? Like *lecture* or *scold*. Actually, the word *exhortation* comes from the same Greek word used for the Holy Spirit, translated "Helper" in the New American Standard Bible, "Counselor" in the New International Version, and "Comforter" in the King James (see John 16:7).[2] From these parallels we can formulate our definition of exhortation. It is the ability

> to bring encouragement,
> to help others see the relevance of Scripture,
> to give insightful counsel,
> to motivate,
> to comfort, and
> to offer hope that prompts action.

Exhortation may seem similar to the support gift of teaching; however, there are at least three important distinctions between the two gifts.

Teacher	Exhorter
Communicates facts clearly and accurately.	Stimulates listener to respond to the facts.
Explains the *what* of Scripture.	Explains the *how* of Scripture.
Gets excited by the truth itself.	Gets excited by the ways truth can make a difference when applied.

Exhorters need to have an uncanny awareness of life's practicalities. They need to know how to apply truth in the home and in the marketplace and how to visualize the steps needed to accomplish those applications. Having great insight into people's needs, they are able to shoot an arrow of truth into a person's heart, while remaining tactful and encouraging.

---

2. Jesus referred to the Holy Spirit as the "Helper," which is a form of the Greek verb *parakaleō*. That same verb is the root of our word translated *exhortation* and literally means "called alongside." One lexicon defines the noun as "called to one's aid in a judicial cause." G. Abbott-Smith, *A Manual Greek Lexicon of the New Testament*, 3d ed. (Edinburgh, Scotland: T. and T. Clark, 1937), p. 340.

A true exhorter can look you square in the eye and confront your sinful wanderings. Such a confrontation may be wounding at first, but the exhorter always knows how to restore your spirit and set you back on God's path (see Prov. 27:6; Gal. 6:1).

Two examples of gifted exhorters in the Bible are Aquila and his wife Priscilla, faithful members of the burgeoning church in Ephesus. One day, a new and powerful teacher, Apollos, came to their city and was speaking boldly about Christ.

> Now a certain Jew named Apollos, an Alexandrian by birth, an eloquent man, came to Ephesus; and he was mighty in the Scriptures. This man had been instructed in the way of the Lord; and being fervent in spirit, he was speaking and teaching accurately the things concerning Jesus, being acquainted only with the baptism of John; and he began to speak out boldly in the synagogue. (Acts 18:24–26a)

Apollos knew the gospel message, but he was unaware of the Holy Spirit's ministry that began after Jesus' ascension. So,

> when Priscilla and Aquila heard him, they took him aside and explained to him the way of God more accurately. (v. 26b)

They exhorted him. Without criticizing or belittling him, this wise couple privately and humbly pointed out his errors in theology. Receiving such correction from anyone less tactful, Apollos could have become embarrassed or defensive. But because of Aquila and Priscilla's encouraging exhortations, Apollos shone even brighter as an eloquent and powerful defender of the gospel of Jesus (see vv. 27–28).

Who are your exhorters? Maybe a discipler, a counselor, a consultant, or a youth worker has shaped you into a shining witness for Christ. Maybe your mother has been the most influential exhorter in your life, for surely many mothers have this gift.

But this is not all that mothers model. In fact, the next gift we will examine—giving—is one of their hallmarks.

The Gift of Giving

Paul encourages those with the gift of giving to give "with liberality" (Rom. 12:8).[3] From this brief description of how one is to give, we can formulate a clear definition of the gift itself. It is *the ability to contribute material resources to the Lord's work with generosity, frequency, and cheerfulness.*

Unlike those with the serving/helping gift who donate their time and energy, givers help the church by donating their money. Many times, they have an uncanny ability to accumulate riches, but that ability never makes them greedy or stingy. Rather, they are remarkably unselfish with their dollars, because they realize that their money is really God's anyway. In addition,

> they don't keep records of who gave what so they can compete,
> they don't grumble when opportunities to give come their way,
> they don't draw public attention to their giving, and
> they don't need to be coerced into giving.

Giving spontaneously, generously, and always with a cheerful attitude, they even shock us sometimes by offering a gift far beyond what was needed or requested. Barnabas is an example of one such giver.

> And Joseph, a Levite of Cyprian birth, who was also called Barnabas by the apostles (which translated means, Son of Encouragement), and who owned a tract of land, sold it and brought the money and laid it at the apostles' feet. (Acts 4:36–37)

Are there Barnabas-type givers in your congregation? Those who willingly contribute extravagantly? Understand them in light of their gift of giving, and be careful not to take advantage of their generosity. On the other hand, don't restrict their giving either. If you open their eyes to the hundreds of worthwhile projects to which they can give, you'll see them come alive as they excitedly give, give, and give some more!

---

3. *Liberality,* from the Greek word *haplotēs,* comes from the root word meaning "singleness." It conveys the idea of giving with "sincerity, generously, liberally. It refers to open-handed and open-hearted giving out of compassion and a singleness of purpose, not from ambition." Fritz Rienecker, *A Linguistic Key to the Greek New Testament* (Grand Rapids, Mich.: Zondervan Publishing House, Regency Reference Library, 1980), p. 376.

Such sacrificial giving describes the selflessness of mothers, since they often go without in order to provide for their children. In addition to the gift of giving, mothers model a third spiritual gift—administration.

The Gift of Administration

Administration is like the two sides of a coin; one side is termed "he who leads" in Romans 12:8, and the other is called "administrations" in 1 Corinthians 12:28. First, let's discuss the concept of administrations.

Although this word may bring images of office work to our minds, in Greek it is a nautical term. Literally, "it refers to the steering of a ship."[4] Administrators calmly guide ministries through dangerous seas, undeterred by thrashing winds above and ominous rocks below. They have the vision to see the goal and the skill to guide people to it.

The second side of this gift is leadership. This word in Greek more specifically means "to stand on the first place, to preside"; and the one who stands in this position of authority is to lead diligently (Rom. 12:8), creatively, with common sense, and, as one commentator says, with "zeal."[5]

In combining these two concepts of administrating and leading, we can derive a definition of this gift: *the ability to organize and lead projects, to see them through from start to finish, while handling people tactfully and providing the vision to keep them at the task.*

One of Paul's closest companions had this gift. Titus was able to bring order to the church by organizing the people to work together (see Titus 1:5).[6] We need such calm guidance in our churches today—guidance that provides organization and vision with generous doses of reliability and responsibility. As board members and ministry leaders, these kinds of administrators serve us well.

Administrators guide us with a mother's firm hand; givers provide for us with a mother's selfless spirit; and exhorters correct us with a mother's wisdom. Each of these spiritual gifts expresses attributes of an ideal mother—one who serves, teaches, and comforts us all at the same time.

---

4. Rienecker, A Linguistic Key, p. 430.

5. Rienecker, A Linguistic Key, p. 376.

6. Paul left Titus in Crete to "set in order" the ministry the Apostle left behind. The Greek word translated "set in order" has the "sense of setting right again what was defective." Titus was "to restore what had fallen into disorder." W. E. Vine, Vine's Expository Dictionary of Old and New Testament Words (Old Tappan, N.J.: Fleming H. Revell Co., 1981), p. 145.

Three Lessons Worth Applying

Do you have one of these spiritual gifts so aptly modeled by mothers? If so, listen to three bits of advice that will assist you as you serve others in the church.

First: *Help given to one person benefits the whole family.* Many times in your service ministry you will find that God directs you to just one person. But after a while, you may begin to think, "Am I spending too much time with this person? Are my efforts worth it?" Although doubts may arise, focusing on one individual is actually the best kind of ministry. Eventually, as that person grows, the entire body of Christ will benefit because of your input (compare 1 Cor. 12:26).

Second: *When you see the least results, your efforts are often the most effective.* You may be pouring your life into a person, giving and giving without much response. Don't despair, for God *is* using you; and even though you cannot see the fruit of your service, He can.

Third: *The extent of your contribution cannot be measured until later.* God looks into the hearts of the people you have served and sees the time, the love, and the encouragement you have given them. The entire scope of benefits gained through your efforts, though, may not be fully realized until later—maybe even after you're gone. God calls you only to serve faithfully, and you must try to leave the rest up to Him.

As we continue our study of the service gifts in the next lesson, keep in mind the image of the mother at the beginning of this chapter. Her song of love for her son stayed strong, even through the tough years. May your heart of service be equally enduring as you quietly minister, tenderly singing your song of love.

 Living Insights

Reflecting on the three gifts we've examined in this chapter, you may feel as if you've entered a splendid garment shop. Each article of clothing is displayed appealingly, but which one is your perfect fit?

- First, try on the gift of exhortation. How do you respond to the truths of the Bible? Does your mind immediately search for applications, or do you enjoy analyzing and deciphering Scripture more?

_____

_____

Think back to a time when you confronted someone who was in the wrong. Were you anxious . . . confident . . . compassionate? What were your inner feelings as you talked to that person?

_____

_____

How was your counsel received? Was the person encouraged or disheartened?

_____

_____

- If this gift doesn't quite fit you, try on the gift of giving next. How do you view opportunities to give money to meet a need? Are you enthusiastic or hesitant? Describe your inner attitude and motivations.

_____

_____

Are you constantly looking for ways to give? Would you rather do this privately, or do you enjoy the praise and attention of others?

_____

_____

- Perhaps this gift also isn't your style. So slip on one more, administration. How do you handle a disorganized situation? Do you immediately step in to straighten and organize? Or are you thrown by all the chaos? Write down how you usually respond.

_____

_____

Do you enjoy planning and completing projects? Do you have vision that ignites others and keeps them going? Describe one or two leadership experiences that illustrate these qualities.

_____

_____

If these three service gifts don't seem to fit you well, you'll find another rack in the following lesson. Maybe one of them will be just your size.

 ## Living Insights

Love undergirds all the spiritual gifts (1 Cor. 13:13). It is the solid beam that runs through the core of each. Without it, the gifted person's service is limp and lifeless.

Consider for a moment the necessity of love in the heart of a mother who models the three gifts we discussed today. How does love strengthen

her exhortations? _____

her giving? _____

her administration? _____

Whether you have these three service gifts or not, you still serve others in some way. If motivated by love, your service in the church family will be as effective as the foundation a loving mother provides for her family.

Before studying any more gifts, let's take some time to meditate on the ways of love—the greatest gift of all. And one that is available to everyone.

> Love is patient, love is kind, and is not jealous; love does not brag and is not arrogant, does not act unbecomingly; it does not seek its own, is not provoked, does not take into account a wrong suffered, does not rejoice in unrighteousness, but rejoices with the truth; bears all things, believes all things, hopes all things, endures all things. Love never fails. (1 Cor. 13:4–8a)

Chapter 6

UNIDENTICAL TWINS
IN THE SAME BODY

Romans 12:3–8; 1 Corinthians 12:7–9

The crowd hushes as the young girl strides to the middle of the Olympic arena. The music begins. And like a released spring, she bounces this way and that, flips, spins, and flies through the air. We are amazed at her gymnastic ability, and we would say that she is a gifted athlete.

A man solemnly walks to center stage and faces the audience. The black-suited musicians behind him strike the first notes of the aria. At his cue, the man opens his mouth and unleashes a rich Caruso tone that bathes the auditorium in glorious sound. We would say that he is a gifted singer.

We would also describe those who can play the piano with remarkable dexterity or brush the canvas with inimitable finesse in the same way. The rest of us may dream of possessing such rare talent, but in reality, only a few are so exceptionally blessed.

But there is another kind of giftedness. This kind is most often found in ordinary places like a neighborhood church or a downtown mission. It may not win any awards or receive the world's applause, but it does produce a thunderous ovation in heaven. And the wonderful part about it is that God issues this giftedness in various forms to *all* His children!

Your God-given ability may be one we've already discussed in our study, so let's take a moment to review what we've learned.

A Brief Review of the Serving Gifts

To begin with, we have discovered what God's gifts are not—flamboyant, show-stopping skills that thrill audiences and entertain royalty. More often, they mirror Paul's words to the Corinthian church:

> For consider your calling, brethren, that there were not many wise according to the flesh, not many mighty, not many noble; but God has chosen the foolish things of the world to shame the wise, and

God has chosen the weak things of the world to shame the things which are strong, and the base things of the world and the despised, God has chosen, the things that are not, that He might nullify the things that are. (1 Cor. 1:26–28)

God has reversed the standard. What the world honors, He ignores. As a result, His gifts are more garden-variety than glitzy. But that doesn't mean they are insignificant. They are, in fact, so vital that Paul discusses them in detail, because he wants all believers to be aware of the precious gifts God has given them (see 12:1–7).

Meaning

What is a spiritual gift? As we defined it in earlier lessons, *it is a God-given ability that allows us to carry out a particular function in the family of God with ease and effectiveness.* This means that God has planted in your soul one or a number of gifts that are perfectly suited to your personality. As you cultivate them, they will flourish into an exciting and fulfilling ministry.

Categories

We have already spent some time searching the New Testament for the lists of gifts, finding four key texts: Romans 12, 1 Corinthians 12, Ephesians 4, and 1 Peter 4. In addition, we found that we could categorize them according to three headings—support, service, and sign.

The first group includes such up-front abilities as apostleship, prophecy, evangelism, pastor-teacher, and teacher. The behind-the-scenes gifts make up the second group, including serving/helping, exhorting, giving, administrating, and the two we will examine more closely in this lesson—mercy and faith. The third group encompasses the supernatural abilities of speaking in and interpreting tongues, performing miracles, and healing the sick.

Examples

Since we are in the midst of examining the service gifts, let's spend a little more time focusing specifically on them. How do they operate in the church? Each one has a unique function and works together with the other gifts for the common good (1 Cor. 12:7). In a sense, they complement one another like cogs and springs in a precision timepiece.

For instance, those who have the gift of administration expertly organize events, lead discussion groups, and serve on committees; while those with the gift of exhortation wisely counsel, encourage, disciple, and confront people. Administration and exhortation—a cog and a spring—delicately balanced and operating in tandem to keep the church ticking.

However, if the gifts become out of balance, if some people think their gifts are more important than others', the church will sputter and its effectiveness will eventually wind down. That's why Paul warns,

> I say to every man among you not to think more highly of himself than he ought to think; but to think so as to have sound judgment, as God has allotted to each a measure of faith. (Rom. 12:3)

Why should we have a proper opinion of ourselves, expressing our gifts humbly yet confidently? Comparing the church to a human body, Paul explains,

> For just as we have many members in one body and all the members do not have the same function, so we, who are many, are one body in Christ, and individually members one of another. (vv. 4–5)

The members of Christ's body may be diverse, but they are still unified. In the church, there are no Lone Rangers, fighting the bad guys and saving the day on their own. The truth is, we need each other.

A Closer Look at Two More Gifts

This truth of interdependency in the body of Christ is illustrated beautifully in the following two service gifts, which, like unidentical twins, are often seen together but are quite different.

Showing Mercy

The first gift is found in Romans 12:8—"he who shows mercy." Those with this gift can sense people's needs and embrace them with comfort, warmth, and hope. They are also exceptionally perceptive of pain and can soothe others with just the right word or touch. And if words or touch are inappropriate, they know how to sit quietly and just let their presence bring hope and encouragement. Those who have endured soul-stabbing despair know the value of such a discerning comforter.

Paul adds an important "how-to" to this gift: "with cheerfulness." One commentator defines this phrase as "the joyful eagerness, the amiable grace, the affability . . . which make the visitor a sunbeam penetrating into the sick-chamber, and to the heart of the afflicted."[1]

One suffering Old Testament saint was not so fortunate as to have a wise mercy-giver at his side. His name was Job, and the so-called friends who came to comfort him broke every rule of showing mercy.

First, they sat and mourned too long—seven days, without a word (Job 2:13). Instead, they should have brought at least a ray of hope. *Second,* when they finally said something, they preached at Job and judged him instead of entering into his pain (4:7–9). *Third,* they argued with him instead of compassionately understanding his doubts (15:2–4). And *fourth,* they added to his pain instead of bringing him relief (19:1–3).

So Job, sitting among the ashes, destitute and alone, received no cup of cool water from his friends—only bitter dregs. "I have heard many such things," he sighed. "Sorry comforters are you all" (16:2).

If Job could counsel us today, he would say, "Watch your words when you try to comfort someone." For as the writer of Proverbs observed,

> There is one who speaks rashly like the thrusts of
> a sword,
> But the tongue of the wise brings healing.
> (12:18; see also 15:4; 25:11–12)

Able to sensitively soothe those in pain, the one who knows what to say and when to say it definitely has a gift from the Lord. Joseph Bayly, who grieved through the loss of three sons, experienced this kind of soothing comfort, as well as the sorry kind. He recalls,

> I was sitting, torn by grief. Someone came and
> talked to me of God's dealings, of why it happened,
> of hope beyond the grave. He talked constantly, he
> said things I knew were true.
>
> I was unmoved, except to wish he'd go away. He
> finally did.

---

1. Marvin R. Vincent, *Word Studies in the New Testament* (McLean, Va.: MacDonald Publishing Co., n.d.), vol. 3, p. 158.

Another came and sat beside me. He didn't talk.
He didn't ask leading questions. He just sat beside
me for an hour and more, listened when I said something, answered briefly, prayed simply, left.
I was moved. I was comforted. I hated to see
him go.[2]

Paul also described one of his comforters, Onesiphorus, as one who
"refreshed me" when he was imprisoned in Rome (2 Tim. 1:15–18).[3]
Like a cool cloth on the forehead, the presence of the mercy-giver
revives those who suffer in hot anguish.

Another gift in the service category also revives others. It is
mercy's unidentical twin—faith.

Faith

In one sense, every Christian has faith in Christ for salvation;
but in 1 Corinthians 12:9, Paul is referring to a faith of a different
kind.[4] We can define this gift as *the ability to discern God's will, pursue
it with extraordinary confidence, and then lay hold of God's promises
with remarkable results.*

Those with this kind of faith are cut from a different cloth than
the rest of us. They can perceive God's will no matter how foggy
it seems to others, claim His presence in the midst of chaos, wait
on Him without a hint of wavering, and then witness God's amazing
results with calm satisfaction instead of surprise.

Paul himself had this gift of faith, which was dramatically illustrated when his ship encountered a sail-shredding storm on his
voyage to Rome. Notice his calm confidence as he shouted to the
crew over the roar of the howling wind.

"I urge you to keep up your courage, for there shall
be no loss of life among you, but only of the ship.

---

2. Joseph Bayly, *The Last Thing We Talk About*, rev. ed. (Elgin, Ill.: David C. Cook Publishing
Co., 1973), pp. 55–56.

3. The Greek word for "refreshed" is *anapsuchō*, which means "to cool again, to cool off."
Kenneth S. Wuest, "The Pastoral Epistles," in *Wuest's Word Studies from the Greek New
Testament* (Grand Rapids, Mich.: William B. Eerdmans Publishing Co., 1979), vol. 2, p. 126.

4. Paul subtly indicates that this is a different kind of faith when he uses the term *heteros*
rather than *allos* for the word "another." *Heteros* specifically denotes "another of a different
kind" while *allos* means "another of the same kind." See also G. Abbott-Smith, *A Manual
Greek Lexicon of the New Testament*, 3d ed. (Edinburgh, Scotland: T. and T. Clark, 1937), p. 22.

For this very night an angel of the God to whom I belong and whom I serve stood before me, saying, 'Do not be afraid, Paul; you must stand before Caesar; and behold, God has granted you all those who are sailing with you.' Therefore, keep up your courage, men, for I believe God, that it will turn out exactly as I have been told." (Acts 27:22–25)

Did the Lord deliver them as Paul believed He would? The ship ran aground on an island, but as Luke's account recalls, "all were brought safely to land" (v. 44).

Like Paul, those who have the gift of faith see God's hand through the storm and trust Him with complete abandon. They are not weird psychic types who peer into crystal balls. Rather, they are levelheaded people of prayer who simply take God at His word. And if you are around them for very long, you'll discover that their faith is contagious. You, too, will begin to see God's light through the clouds.

A Personal Application Worth Considering

These twin gifts of mercy and faith, like the rest of the service gifts, may be quiet, but they are essential in bringing comfort, reassurance, and hope to the body of Christ. So if you have either of these gifts—or any service gift—keep in mind your crucial role in the church and these two words of advice.

First: *Your gift is a privilege; so accept it, but don't flaunt it.* Have sound judgment concerning your gift by recognizing your abilities and understanding your limitations at the same time.

. Second: *Your gift is a responsibility; so use it, but don't abuse it.* God's gift to you comes with a serious warning label. You are responsible to use His gift, but you must do so with love. Administrators should lead with love, exhorters should reprove with love—love should accompany all the gifts. For without it, we can easily abuse and manipulate others instead of building them up for the common good.

 ## Living Insights STUDY ONE

In the book *When Life Isn't Fair,* Dr. Dwight Carlson cites several medical studies which prove that by showing mercy, you can help someone with a serious illness live longer. Interestingly, companionship during suffering is healing medicine for the soul *and* the body.[5]

Do you think you might have this life-giving gift of showing mercy? Let the following questions help you decide.

Do you have the ability to sense when a person is in need even before they tell you? Describe a time when this occurred.

_____

_____

When you are with people in emotional or physical pain, how do you respond? Are you drawn closer to them? Write down your usual reactions.

_____

_____

Think back on a time when you were with a person in deep need. Did you seem to know when to be quiet, when to speak, what to say, and what not to say? Describe the situation, what you said to the person, and how they responded.

_____

_____

Now focus on showing mercy's twin gift, faith. Do you think you might have this equally vital gift?

When a problem arises that seems an impossibility, is your initial response pessimistic? Or are you expectant, looking forward to how God will handle this situation?

_____

_____

When diverging roads appear before you, are you able to see God's path based on His Word in a way that others miss? If so,

5. Dwight Carlson and Susan Carlson Wood, *When Life Isn't Fair* (Eugene, Oreg.: Harvest House Publishers, 1989), pp. 141–42.

describe a recent situation when you felt confident about God's will. What were the results of your faith in this situation? Did the Lord come through in a remarkable way?

_____

_____

_____

 ## Living Insights

"But what do I say?" This is often the response of those who fear visiting a suffering person. Dr. Dwight Carlson and his daughter Susan give us some helpful tips to reduce that fear.

• First, keep in mind the stages of suffering. These phases are denial and isolation, anger, bargaining, depression, and acceptance.[6] Be understanding as your friend goes through each stage.

• Second, prepare yourself for the visit by evaluating your own feelings. Also find out the best time to come by and what your friend's greatest needs are emotionally or physically.

• Third, avoid statements like "Things could be worse", "You can still have more children", "It was God's will", "It was for the best", "Time will heal", or "God knows what He is doing." All these may be true, but they tend to negate or criticize your friend's feelings.

• Fourth, a sincere "I'm sorry" followed by a touch or a hug are often the best things to say and do. Share your feelings. Let your friend know how much you care and how deeply you hurt for them. Many times, you don't have to say anything—just your presence brings comfort.

• Fifth, rather than saying, "Let me know if I can do anything for you," offer to help in specific and practical ways.[7]

Following this advice, you can be an angel of mercy to those you love.

6. See Elisabeth Kübler-Ross, On Death and Dying (New York, N.Y.: Macmillan Publishing Co., 1969).

7. Based on Carlson and Wood, When Life Isn't Fair, pp. 186–98.

Chapter 7

WHAT ABOUT MIRACLES AND HEALING TODAY?

Acts 3:1–16

So far, our study of spiritual gifts has been pretty safe and predictable—helping, teaching, and showing mercy aren't very risky realms for discussion. But as we cross over into the sign or "charismatic" gifts, the terrain changes.[1] We must proceed carefully here; for unfortunately, this area has often become a mine field of controversy.

We can trace this volatility to two basic causes, extremism and experience.

Extremism. Some noncharismatic Christians go so far as to say that the supernatural acts of healing, miracles, and tongues are actually the work of Satan. On the other end of the spectrum, some charismatic Christians embarrass mainstream charismatics with behavior such as handling poisonous snakes and refusing medical care for their children, and with claims of lengthened legs, miraculously filled teeth, and so forth.

Each extreme promotes damaging caricatures of the other, with noncharismatics presented as devoid of emotion and charismatics portrayed as all emotion. Both caricatures are untrue, unfair, and inappropriate.

Experience. Another reason for conflict concerns the issue of subjective experience and the Bible. Some emphasize Scripture to the exclusion of experience, a position that comes dangerously close to treating Scripture as a cold, academic textbook. Assuredly, we should strive to understand the Bible literally and interpret each verse within its context—a process that takes study and effort. But we must also make God's Word live in our hearts, where it is meant to be.

---

1. *Charismatic* comes from the Greek word *charisma*, which simply means "gift." See Walter Bauer, *A Greek-English Lexicon of the New Testament*, trans. William F. Arndt and F. Wilbur Gingrich, 2d. ed., rev. (Chicago, Ill.: University of Chicago Press, 1979), p. 878. Today the term is associated with those who promote the expression of such spiritual gifts as miracles, healing, and speaking in tongues. See Bruce Barron, *The Health and Wealth Gospel* (Downers Grove, Ill.: InterVarsity Press, 1987), pp. 10–11.

On the other hand, our experiences should never be believed *over* Scripture. Our faith needs to be based on truth, and there is no more solid bedrock of truth than God's inspired Word. Also, while miraculous experiences are impressive, the pursuit of them can carry us away from what is central to God's Word—the Cross. Paul addressed this problem when he wrote to the church in Corinth.

> For indeed Jews ask for signs, and Greeks search for wisdom; but we preach Christ crucified, to Jews a stumbling block, and to Gentiles foolishness.
> (1 Cor. 1:22–23)

Like those Jews, we sometimes crave tantalizing signs to bolster our faith. The promise of miracles can draw huge crowds, but the spectacular was not Jesus' style; His focus was the Cross and our salvation (see Matt. 12:38–41; John 6:30–35). William Barclay provides some helpful background that explains why the Jews stumbled over the nonspectacular Jesus.

> The Jew sought for signs. When the golden age of God came he looked for startling happenings. This very time during which Paul was writing produced a crop of false Messiahs, and all of them had beguiled the people into accepting them by the promise of wonders. In A.D. 45 a man called Theudas had emerged. He had persuaded thousands of the people to abandon their homes and follow him out to the Jordan, by promising that, at his word of command, the Jordan would divide and he would lead them dryshod across. In A.D. 54 a man from Egypt arrived in Jerusalem, claiming to be the Prophet. He persuaded thirty thousand people to follow him out to the Mount of Olives by promising that at his word of command the walls of Jerusalem would fall down. That was the kind of thing that the Jews were looking for. In Jesus they saw one who was meek and lowly, one who deliberately avoided the spectacular, one who served and who ended on a Cross—and it seemed to them an impossible picture of the Chosen One of God.[2]

2. William Barclay, *The Letters to the Corinthians*, rev. ed., The Daily Study Bible Series (Philadelphia, Pa.: Westminster Press, 1975), p. 18.

We must be wary of making the same mistakes the Jews made—following teachers who spout grandiose promises they may not be able to keep. Instead, we need to follow Jesus and the simple, humble way of His cross.

So as we enter the challenging terrain of the sign gifts, let's keep in mind the dangers of going to extremes and valuing experience too much or too little. Let's open the Scriptures—our most reliable map—and objectively analyze God's Word and practice it. We'll start our exploration by gaining an understanding of some key terms.

Understanding Several Important Terms

The following three words and their definitions will help us get our footing as we begin our in-depth study, a study that will carry through the next two lessons.

Signs

We have labeled this category of gifts as the "sign gifts." *Sign* simply means an identifying mark; but in Scripture, it also means an attesting act that verified that someone was from God.[3] Jesus proved that He was the Son of God partially through miraculous signs—many of which were not even recorded in the Gospel accounts (John 20:30–31).

So, when we refer to a sign gift, we are talking about *a superhuman ability which authenticated God's spokespersons by convincing people that they were, in fact, bona fide servants of God* (see also 1 Cor. 14:22).

Why were these gifts necessary? Well, remember, first-century Christians had access only to the Old Testament scrolls—the New Testament was not yet completed. So if a teacher stood up proclaiming right and wrong, the people needed some way of knowing that the person and the message were from God. The sign gifts helped them determine who was authentic and which teaching they could trust.

One way teachers such as Paul validated their ministry was through performing miracles, our next term to define.

---

3. *Sign* comes from the Greek word, *semeion*, which means a "*distinguishing mark* by which something is known, *token, indication.*" In Luke 2:12, the newborn Jesus was distinguished as the "baby wrapped in cloths, and lying in a manger." In certain contexts, this word means "a wonder or miracle, an event that is contrary to the usual course of nature." In 2 Corinthians 12:12, true apostles were distinguished from false teachers "by signs and wonders and miracles." Bauer, Arndt, and Gingrich, *Greek-English Lexicon*, pp. 747, 748.

Miracles

To fully grasp what miracles are, it is important to understand what they are not. They are not events that are natural, improbable, or merely unusual. Finding a close parking space at the mall right before Christmas may be improbable, but it is not a miracle. Winning a race when you started out dead last may be remarkable, but it isn't miraculous.

Miracles defy natural reasoning; *they are extraordinary, unexplainable events that manifest supernatural power.* They have only two possible sources: God and Satan. And since both God and Satan exist, miracles can and do happen.

Scripture describes many miraculous events, but these miracles had a well-defined role. Their purpose was never to draw a crowd or to draw attention to a person; rather, they were to bring people to faith in God.[4]

Jesus performed miracles to inspire faith (Matt. 8:23–27), but knowing that human nature tends to crave the sensational, He often refused when challenged to conjure up a miraculous sign (Mark 8:11–13). Many of Jesus' miracles involved curing an illness or disability, which brings us to our third term.

Healings

The healings Jesus performed, like all healings described in Scripture, occurred apart from the natural process that takes place when you recover from an operation or a sprained ankle. Rather, biblical healings were *immediate and complete physical or mental restorations that circumvented or interrupted natural laws.* An example of such a supernatural healing is found in Acts 3.

> Now Peter and John were going up to the temple at the ninth hour, the hour of prayer. And a certain man who had been lame from his mother's womb was being carried along, whom they used to set down every day at the gate of the temple which is called Beautiful, in order to beg alms of those who were entering the temple. And when he saw Peter and John about to go into the temple, he began asking to receive alms. And Peter, along with John, fixed

---

4. Interestingly, when Moses attempted to draw attention to himself through a miracle, God disciplined him (Num. 20:8–12).

his gaze upon him and said, "Look at us!" And he began to give them his attention, expecting to receive something from them. But Peter said, "I do not possess silver and gold, but what I do have I give to you: In the name of Jesus Christ the Nazarene—walk!" And seizing him by the right hand, he raised him up; and immediately his feet and his ankles were strengthened. And with a leap, he stood upright and began to walk; and he entered the temple with them, walking and leaping and praising God. (vv. 1–8)

Was there a process? Did the lame man hobble along for a few days, slowly feeling strength return to his feeble legs? No, he "leaped" into the air, his brittle bones and severed tendons revitalizing in an instant, his atrophied muscles and cemented joints coming to life! Peter explained this phenomenon later to the skeptical Jewish leaders:

"And on the basis of faith in His name, it is the name of Jesus which has strengthened this man whom you see and know; and the faith which comes through Him has given him this perfect health in the presence of you all." (v. 16)

As everyone present could testify, God supernaturally and instantaneously gave this once-lame beggar perfect health. So we can say with confidence that miraculous healing in the Bible has nothing to do with any natural process.

Also from this passage, we can conclude that biblical healing depends solely on God and has nothing to do with the power of any human being. Peter made this point emphatically clear when he said, "It is the name of Jesus which has strengthened this man."

Furthermore, we can see that biblical healing has nothing to do with who has how much faith, for the lame man wasn't even expecting to be healed, let alone trying to muster up enough faith to accomplish it. Healing is ultimately determined by God's will, not the degree of our faith.[5]

---

5. In Mark 9:20–27, a demon-possessed boy was brought to Jesus. The boy's father pleaded with Jesus, saying, "If You can do anything, take pity on us and help us!" But Jesus perceived doubt in the father's words and replied, " 'If You can!' All things are possible to him who believes." To this the father responded, "I do believe, help my unbelief." Then Jesus cast out the demon in the boy; but notice, He did so even though the father admitted he had weak faith.

Recognizing a Few Crucial Facts

Several more crucial principles from the whole of Scripture will guide us in understanding God's use of signs, miracles, and healings. First: *God's great eras began with great displays of miracles.* Theologian John Stott gives us a whirlwind tour of a few of these ages.

> Certainly the thrust of the Bible is that miracles clustered round the principal . . . epochs of revelation, particularly Moses the lawgiver, the new prophetic witness spearheaded by Elijah and Elisha, the Messianic ministry of Jesus, and the apostles, so that Paul referred to his miracles as "the things that mark an apostle" [2 Cor. 12:12].[6]

And, as we said before, these signs revealed God's power, authenticated His witnesses, and inspired faith (see also 2 Kings 5:1–15).

Second: *As each era got underway, miracles faded.* So often we center our attention on the brief periods when God broke the natural laws with His astounding wonders. But when you examine Scripture as a whole, you will notice that long periods of time occur when God's miracles are absent. After He had launched a new era and it was well underway, He withdrew His signs and they became rarer and rarer until they faded away.[7]

Third: *To say the sign gifts have served their purpose does not mean that all miracles and healings have ceased.* Simply because God has stopped issuing the sign gifts to men and women today does not mean that He has stopped performing miracles. We should pray for healing; we should pray for miracles. God is our divine Healer, and we can come to Him knowing that He will hear our prayer (Heb. 4:16).

Remembering Some Significant Distinctions

In the next lesson, we will explore more deeply how we pray for healing today. But for now, let's summarize this chapter by reviewing three key distinctions.

---

6. John Stott, *The Spirit, the Church, and the World: The Message of Acts* (Downers Grove, Ill.: InterVarsity Press, 1990), p. 102.

7. Further biblical and historical support that the sign gifts have ceased is found in William McRae's book *Dynamics of Spiritual Gifts* (Grand Rapids, Mich.: Zondervan Publishing House, 1976), pp. 90–99; and in Thomas R. Edgar's article, "The Cessation of the Sign Gifts," *Bibliotheca Sacra*, October–December 1988, pp. 371–86.

One, God-ordained miracles are not commonplace, and they never result in human glory. When that rare miracle comes along, a true test of the source of it is who gets the attention, who gets the glory; God-ordained miracles should result in God-glorifying faith. Two, God-ordained healings are rare, and when they occur, they are unquestionable. When God heals someone, the healing will pass any test and stand up to any investigation. And three, neither miracles or healings are as convincing as the Scriptures. Jesus Himself taught this in His story of the rich man and Lazarus the beggar.

After both men had died, the rich man pleaded with Abraham to send Lazarus to warn his brothers of God's impending wrath. But Abraham said, "If they do not listen to Moses and the Prophets, neither will they be persuaded if someone rises from the dead" (Luke 16:31).

As we continue handling this hotly contended subject of the sign gifts in the pages to come, especially keep that last thought in mind. *Scripture* is the persuasive tool that turns the hearts of skeptics, not signs and wonders. So focus your eyes on God's Word—the light to guide your way.

 Living Insights

The wise nineteenth-century preacher Charles Haddon Spurgeon once observed,

> It is not likely we should all see eye to eye. You cannot make a dozen watches all tick to the same time, much less make a dozen men all think the same thoughts.[8]

This is particularly true in regard to the sign gifts. You may not see eye to eye with a friend or relative concerning these gifts, but still you are both members of Christ's body, brothers and sisters in the faith.

Right on the heels of Paul's discussion of the spiritual gifts in Romans 12:1–8 is a passage on relationships in the church. Coincidence? Maybe Paul realized the volatile nature of the gifts, so he

---

8. Charles H. Spurgeon, *Spurgeon at His Best*, comp. Tom Carter (Grand Rapids, Mich.: Baker Book House, 1988), p. 32.

balanced them with instructions on how to get along with one another. If followed, his words will stock the shelves of your heart with loving attitudes that should pad your relationships when differences arise.

Read Romans 12:9–21. Do you see any commands that particularly apply to how you should relate to someone with whom you have a difference of opinion? Write them down.

_____ _____

_____ _____

_____ _____

_____ _____

Now plan ways you can put some of these into practice—starting today!

_____

_____

_____

_____

_____

 ## Living Insights STUDY TWO

Water tastes best at its source, in the mountains where streams glisten and gurgle as they flow, swirling in little pools that are as clear and cool as the air itself. But as inviting as these cascading streams may be, wise hikers always use a special filter to purify the water before they drink it.

Subjective experiences with the sign gifts may look as appealing as a rocky mountain stream, and we may long to drink them in. But as hikers along God's path, we must be careful to pour our experiences through a purifying filter—His Word.

You can start this filtering process by reading about those who had the gifts of miracles and healing in the book of Acts. In the space provided, write down some characteristics of their healing

60

ministry—such as the setting, the method, the results, and the response.

Peter (3:1–10; 5:14–16) _____

_____

_____

Philip (8:4–8) _____

_____

_____

Paul (19:8–12) _____

_____

_____

If you are familiar with the ministries of faith healers today, do you see any similarities or differences between them and the ministries of these men in the book of Acts? Write down your comparisons.

_____

_____

_____

If the methods and results of modern faith healers vary from those of the gifted men in Acts, you should beware of possible impurities. Filtering contemporary ministries through the grid of Scripture will help you determine which teaching to believe and which church to attend. But mostly, it will guide you to ministries that are producing cool, clear, pure truth to refresh you on your spiritual journey.

Chapter 8

A CALM, SCRIPTURAL ANALYSIS OF HEALING

1 Corinthians 12:10, 28–30; James 5:13–16

Feeling like a prisoner in her own body, Rita longed to be free from the iron chains of her cerebral palsy. One night, her Christian friends gathered around her, saying, "If you just have faith, Rita, God will enable you to walk."

"If you just have faith"—the words echoed in her mind. *If I just have faith.* She shut her eyes tightly, and the small group prayed with all their might.

When the praying ceased, all eyes focused on Rita. She grasped the armrests of the wheelchair and slowly lifted herself up. Her heart bursting with hope, she took one step, then two, three, four . . . twenty steps before stumbling. The group cheered and promised her that if she continued to believe God, her healing would soon be complete.

She did believe God in the days that followed. But her healing never came. Desperately, she tried and tried, but she couldn't even repeat her triumphant steps from that first hopeful night.

Had God forsaken her? Did He want her to remain chained to her wheelchair? Was her disease a result of some sin in her life? Was her faith just not strong enough?[1]

Every person, healthy or sick, has asked similar questions—questions that well up when diseases go unchecked and prayers seem to go unanswered. There is a place, though, where we can bring them: the Word of God. Let's open up this Guide and examine its answers about two pertinent spiritual gifts, working miracles and healing.

A Careful Explanation of Two Sign Gifts

In the previous lesson, we pried open the topic of miracles and healing in general. Now we will examine the specific gifts of performing miracles and healing to which Paul referred in 1 Corinthians 12:7–10, 28–29.

---

1. Rita's story is found in Bruce Barron's *The Health and Wealth Gospel* (Downers Grove, Ill.: InterVarsity Press, 1987), pp. 5–6.

The Gift of Working Miracles

In New Testament times, the gift of working miracles was God's seal of approval on a person's ministry, proving that His presence and authority rested on that person's words and actions (see 2 Cor. 12:12). We can define this gift, then, as *the superhuman ability to interrupt or alter natural laws for the purpose of displaying God's supernatural power and presence.*

Also, these God-empowered miracles sparked two reactions that aided the growth and well-being of the early church: (1) unsaved people believed in the message of the gospel, and (2) Christians could recognize and therefore trust God's authentic messengers.

To see this gift of miracles at work, we need only to turn to Paul and Barnabas. On their first missionary journey, when Paul was still known as Saul, they encountered a Jewish magician named Bar-Jesus who was determined to keep the local proconsul, Sergius Paulus, from trusting Christ (Acts 13:4–8). So Paul performed a miracle that blinded the magician but opened Sergius Paulus' eyes so that he believed the gospel, "being amazed at the teaching of the Lord" (vv. 9–12). Not "amazed at the power of Paul," notice; still, through the miracle, this man's eyes were turned to God.[2]

The Gift of Performing Healings

The next gift we'll look at is healing, which is *the superhuman ability to restore health immediately and completely for the purpose of displaying God's power and presence.*

As with miracles, healing should emphasize divine power, not human expertise. Paul and Barnabas again provide a good example. While ministering in Lystra, they encountered a man who had been lame from birth. So Paul healed him, and immediately "he leaped up and began to walk" (Acts 14:8–10). As a result of the miracle, the people glorified them instead of God, believing that they were the Greek gods Hermes and Zeus become men (vv. 11–13). It was a truly exasperating situation for Paul and Barnabas.

> But when the apostles, Barnabas and Paul, heard of it, they tore their robes and rushed out into the crowd, crying out and saying, "Men, why are you doing these things? We are also men of the same

---

2. See also Acts 14:1–4 for an example of miracles as a sign that validated Paul's ministry.

nature as you, and preach the gospel to you in order that you should turn from these vain things to a living God, who made the heaven and the earth and the sea, and all that is in them. . . . He did not leave Himself without witness, in that He did good and gave you rains from heaven and fruitful seasons, satisfying your hearts with food and gladness." (vv. 14–15, 17)

Rather than basking in the false glory of the moment, Paul and Barnabas instead shifted the focus to the Lord, presenting the gospel message of a loving God. This should be our attitude too, if God happens to work in wonderful ways through us.

Now that we have a foundational understanding of this gift, we are ready to build a view of how God heals today. For although He no longer issues the sign gifts of miracle-working and healing, He Himself still alters natural law and superhumanly heals diseases.[3]

As we proceed with our study, remember that, in saying these gifts aren't for today, we are in no way weakening our faith in God. We may be putting less trust in faith healers, but certainly not in our Lord. His workings do not depend on the gifts of men and women but only upon His sovereign right and power.

An In-Depth Examination of Healing

To help us skillfully construct God's perspective on healing, let's first nail down a few points of basic theology.[4]

Foundational Facts to Remember regarding Sin and Sickness

First: *There are two categories of sin—original and personal.* Original sin refers to the sin nature we inherited from Adam (Rom. 5:12), while personal sin is the daily disobedience that is spawned by our Adamic nature (3:23). Original sin is the root; personal sin is the fruit.

Want an example? Think of children. As beautiful and innocent as youngsters are, they never have to be taught to do wrong, do they?

---

3. Since we have God's complete revelation in the Bible, we no longer need miracles as authenticating signs of God's Word. However, "Jesus Christ is the same yesterday and today, yes and forever" (Heb. 13:8), and He still works miracles and performs healings.

4. This section is based on "Suffering, Sickness, Sin—and Healing," from the study guide *James: Practical and Authentic Living,* coauthored by Lee Hough, from the Bible-teaching ministry of Charles R. Swindoll (Fullerton, Calif.: Insight for Living, 1991).

They, and we, have a propensity in our nature to do wrong, which reflects our legacy from Adam; and our personal sins come from choosing to spend and invest this inheritance.

Second: *Original sin introduced sickness and death to the human race.* Romans 5:12 states:

> Therefore, just as through one man sin entered into the world, and death through sin, and so death spread to all men, because all sinned.

Had Adam and Eve never sinned, they would never have died. But because they disobeyed God, sickness and death spread to every living thing. So, in the broadest sense, all sickness and death are the result of original sin.

Third: *Sometimes there is a direct relationship between personal sin and sickness.* Remember the story of David and Bathsheba in 2 Samuel 11–12? David committed adultery with Bathsheba, arranged for her husband to be killed, then refused to acknowledge his sin. Finally, after a rebuke from the prophet Nathan, David confessed and repented. Psalm 32 is David's journal of this period. It reveals the physical sufferings he experienced while denying his sin.

> When I kept silent about my sin, my body wasted away
> Through my groaning all day long.
> For day and night Thy hand was heavy upon me;
> My vitality was drained away as with the fever
>   heat of summer.
> (vv. 3–4; see also 38:5–7)

Fourth: *Other times there is no relationship between personal sin and sickness.*[5] Once when the disciples and Jesus passed by a blind man, they asked,

> "Rabbi, who sinned, this man or his parents, that he should be born blind?" Jesus answered, "It was neither that this man sinned, nor his parents; but it was in order that the works of God might be displayed in him." (John 9:2b–3; see also Acts 3:2–8)

---

5. If all our sickness resulted from personal sin, then one would think that we need only to confess those sins to be healed. Also, Jesus would not need to sympathize with us in our "infirmities," as He does, if our sickness was caused by sin (see Heb. 4:15 KJV); He would simply exhort us to repent.

Fifth: *It is not God's will that everyone be healed.* Usually, those who claim that it is God's will for everyone to be healed base their belief upon the last phrase of Isaiah 53:5b, "And by His scourging we are healed." However, the context of this verse refers to spiritual illness and healing, not physical, as the apostle Peter makes clear.

> And He Himself bore our sins in His body on the cross, that we might die to sin and live to righteousness; for by His wounds you were healed. (1 Pet. 2:24).

Also, it is noteworthy that even though the apostle Paul had the gift of healing, he left Trophimus sick in Miletus (2 Tim. 4:20); his friend Epaphroditus almost died while ministering to him (Phil. 2:25–27); and Timothy, his spiritual son, had an ongoing stomach problem and "frequent ailments" (1 Tim. 5:23). Paul even asked God three times to remove his own "thorn in the flesh" (2 Cor. 12:7–8). But God said, "My grace is sufficient for you" (v. 9)—in other words, *"It is not My will that you be healed."*

Biblical Guidelines to Follow regarding Sickness and Healing

With these five facts to build upon, let's listen now to the words of another New Testament writer, James, who gives instructions to those who are afflicted or sick.

Dealing with personal weaknesses and afflictions. James addresses this category in the fifth chapter of his epistle: "Is anyone among you suffering? Let him pray" (v. 13a).

The Greek term for *suffering* here literally means "in distress." It's a broad term that can mean a general affliction from which there is no immediate relief. James tells this person, "Pray!" He doesn't promise that if we pray we will be healed; rather, it's as if he is exhorting us to pray for endurance through the affliction.

Finding relief from certain physical and mental illnesses. In verse 14, James introduces his second issue.

> Is anyone among you sick? Let him call for the elders of the church, and let them pray over him, anointing him with oil in the name of the Lord.

The Greek term for *sick* used here means "without strength." It is the idea of being totally incapacitated. James recommends three steps in this situation.

First, the sick person should take the initiative to make the illness known. The Greek indicates that those who are sick should summon the elders. James doesn't instruct them to call for a spiri-tually gifted healer, just the spiritual leaders of the church.

Second, the elders are to perform two functions: anoint and pray. According to the Greek sentence structure, verse 14 actually states, "Let them pray over him, *having* anointed him with oil in the name of the Lord." Therefore, the anointing should precede the praying. Typically, the word *anoint* is associated with a religious ceremony where oil is applied to the head (see 1 Sam. 10:1). But as Jay Adams points out in his book *Competent to Counsel,*

> James did not write about ceremonial anointing at all. . . . The ordinary word for a ceremonial anoint-ing was *chrio* (a cognate of *christos* [Christ] the "anointed One"). The word James used (aleipho), in contrast to the word *chrio* ("to anoint"), usually means "to rub" or simply "apply." The word *aleipho* was used to describe the personal application of salves, lotions, and perfumes, which usually had an oil base. . . . An *aleiptes* was a "trainer" who rubbed down athletes in a gymnastic school. *Aleipho* was used frequently in medical treatises. And so it turns out that what James required by the use of oil was the use of the best medical means of the day.[6]

Fortunately, our medical expertise has improved from oil to antibiotics, X rays, and laser surgery. And just as the elders in James' day were to see that proper medical treatment was applied, the same is true of elders today.

Third, the specific results are to be left in the Lord's hands. After anointing, the elders were to pray "in the name of the Lord" (James 5:14b), which means asking God's will for the situation (comp. Luke 22:42). The elders prayed for healing, yet they ac-knowledged God's ultimate sovereignty over the situation.

That prayer of faith leads to three specific results, according to verse 15 of James 5: restoration, raising up, and forgiveness.

> And the prayer offered in faith will restore the one who is sick, and the Lord will raise him up, and if he has committed sins, they will be forgiven him.

6. Jay E. Adams, *Competent to Counsel* (Grand Rapids, Mich.: Baker Book House, 1970), pp. 107–8. Compare Mark 16:1 and John 12:3, regarding ceremonial anointing, with the story of the Good Samaritan in Luke 10:33–34, which refers to medical anointing.

When the person's sickness *is* a result of sin, which apparently is the case here, God will answer the elder's prayers according to His will. He will restore fellowship with the sick person (see v. 20), heal the person physically, and graciously forgive the person's sins.

Practical Points to Keep in Mind

James sums up his instructions on ministering to the sick in verse 16:

> Therefore, confess your sins to one another, and pray for one another, so that you may be healed. The effective prayer of a righteous man can accomplish much.

So as we conclude our study, we can glean four practical measures to follow—two from this verse and two from our passage as a whole.

First: *Praying for one another is essential—practice it!* Your prayers "can accomplish much" on behalf of those you love when you lift them up to our powerful and gracious Lord.

Second: *Use of medical assistance is needed—obey it!* Many times God chooses to heal us naturally instead of supernaturally, and He uses those who are a part of the healing profession to accomplish His will. For anyone who is sick, seeking medical care is essential.

Third: *Confession of sin is healthy—employ it!* Don't let sins build up to the point that they make you physically ill. Apply liberal doses of confession regularly to guard against this possibility.

Fourth: *When healing comes from the Lord—claim it!* Whether or not an illness is the result of personal sin, when God heals, remember to thank Him and give Him the glory!

A Final Word

To those countless Ritas who are confined to braces, wheelchairs, or hospital beds—as well as all of us who live in this sin-sick world—there is hope. However, it is not found in presumptuous promises made by faith healers. It is found in the compelling promise made by the Healer of our souls:

> And I heard a loud voice from the throne, saying, "Behold, the tabernacle of God is among men, and He shall dwell among them, and they shall be His people, and God Himself shall be among them, and He shall wipe away every tear from their eyes; and

there shall no longer be any death; there shall no longer be any mourning, or crying, or pain; the first things have passed away." (Rev. 21:3–4)

Until then, we believe and we wait.

 ## Living Insights

An emotional earthquake occurs whenever disease strikes a family member or friend. Normal life jolts and teeters; its once secure foundation pitches and rocks. Hospital trips, tense phone calls, and tearful embraces become a new, painful norm.

During this crisis period, which may last for weeks or even years, James gives us an emergency kit to open. In the lesson, we discovered its contents in the form of three commands to follow:

1. Make your illness known and call for the spiritual leaders of your church.
2. Ask the elders to pray for you, and seek the best available medical care.
3. Trust the Lord for the results, whether He brings healing or allows pain.

If you or your loved one is in physical distress, have you taken these steps? If you haven't, what do you need to do to take them?

_____

_____

_____

_____

Open your emergency kit soon—through it God will calm your fears and stop your shaking.

 ## Living Insights

Although Scripture clearly teaches that not all illness is caused by personal sins, sometimes runaway sin, as in David's life (2 Sam. 11–12), can bring on physical problems. Write down a description of David's physical condition, found in Psalms 32:3–4 and 38:1–12, that resulted from his unconfessed sin.

_____

_____

_____

_____

We know today that stress brought on by sinful behaviors or attitudes such as extramarital affairs, lying, drunkenness, greed, bitterness, or uncontrolled anger can produce symptoms like back pain, ulcers, and even high blood pressure. If you are experiencing these types of problems, maybe unresolved sin is the true cause. In that case, medical care can treat your symptoms, but only through confession can you treat the source. Spend some time confessing any sins that may be at the root of your illness.

> I acknowledged my sin to Thee,
> And my iniquity I did not hide;
> I said, "I will confess my transgressions to the
>   Lord";
> And Thou didst forgive the guilt of my sin.
> (Ps. 32:5)

Chapter 9

THE GIFT OF SPEAKING IN TONGUES

Acts 2:1–11; 1 Corinthians 14

The gift of speaking in tongues has been called "the biggest Christian friendship and oneness buster of the century."[1] Churches split, friends part company, and families feud—all because of the wide-ranging differences of opinion on speaking in tongues.

As we turn to God's Word concerning this spiritual gift, we don't want to be gathering knowledge just to fortify the armaments of our opinions. Rather, we must commit ourselves at the outset to submitting to love's rule. For as the apostle Paul wrote, "Knowledge makes arrogant, but love edifies" (1 Cor. 8:1b).

So let's endeavor to use our knowledge about tongues as a means to accomplishing love's goals—the building up of one another and the spreading of the gospel. This was, after all, what the gift of tongues was for . . . back when it all began.

The First Occurrence of the Gift of Tongues

The world first heard the miracle of tongues from the mouth of the newborn church.

When and Where

Our historical setting is first-century Jerusalem. The mournful darkness enshrouding Christ's trials and crucifixion had been broken by the triumphant glory of Easter and the awesome wonder of the ascension. Left in the wake of these events were Jesus' amazed followers, who were given the enormous task of being His witnesses "even to the remotest part of the earth" (Acts 1:8b).

How were these few disciples supposed to spread the gospel beyond their little corner of the world? God alone knew, and He had it planned perfectly.

1. George Mallone, *Those Controversial Gifts* (Downers Grove, Ill.: InterVarsity Press, 1983), p. 79.

Just a few days after the Ascension, the Jewish holiday of Pentecost arrived.[2] Jews from all over the world, speaking a smorgasbord of languages, had gathered for this feast, and the city hummed with activity and excitement.

In a certain house in the midst of this hubbub, the remnant of Christ's followers prayed and waited together. It was the ideal moment—with the world at their door—for the rapid dissemination of the gospel. So God looked at His waiting people and said, "Now!"

What and Why

And suddenly there came from heaven a noise like a violent, rushing wind, and it filled the whole house where they were sitting. And there appeared to them tongues as of fire distributing themselves, and they rested on each one of them. And they were all filled with the Holy Spirit and began to speak with other tongues, as the Spirit was giving them utterance.

Now there were Jews living in Jerusalem, devout men, from every nation under heaven. And when this sound occurred, the multitude came together, and were bewildered, because they were each one hearing them speak in his own language.[3]

(Acts 2:2–6)

Speaking in languages other than their own, Christ's newly empowered followers stepped out into the busy, cosmopolitan streets and proclaimed the good news of Christ in words that *everybody* could understand (vv. 7–11).

From these remarkable events at Pentecost, we can formulate a definition of speaking in tongues. It is *the ability to speak in a known language and dialect that has never been studied or learned, with the goal*

---

2. The Feast of Pentecost was also called "the Feast of Harvest" (Exod. 23:16), a fitting backdrop for God to begin His worldwide harvest of souls.

3. There is a Greek word for *unknown*, but it is not used here. Instead, the Greek word used to describe *other tongues* is *heteros*, which, as you may recall from chapter 6, means "another of a different kind." This means that the disciples weren't speaking in unknown languages but in already known languages that were foreign to them. *Language* (vv. 6, 8) in Greek is *dialektos*, which means "dialect of a particular country or district." So they were enabled to speak not only foreign languages but also their unique dialects. G. Abbott-Smith, *A Manual Greek Lexicon of the New Testament*, 3d ed. (Edinburgh, Scotland: T. and T. Clark, 1937), pp. 22 and 109.

of *rapidly disseminating the gospel into nations and cultures that have never heard about Christ.*

We categorize tongues as one of the sign gifts because back then, prior to the completion of the New Testament, it was a sign to unbelievers that God was speaking. And for a few decades after Pentecost, this gift remained a vital part of the first Christian churches. Unfortunately, though, those who possessed this gift sometimes misused or abused it. This was the case in the church at Corinth.

An Evaluation of Tongues . . . Compared to Prophecy

The apostle Paul wrote to the Corinthian church in response to several disturbing problems that had arisen, one of them involving speaking in tongues. In counseling the church members on the proper use of this gift, Paul employed a wise, calm, and logical approach that courses its way from chapter 12 to chapter 14 of 1 Corinthians.

In chapter 12, he begins by listing the spiritual gifts in verses 8–10; and then he returns to this list in verses 29–30, only here he purposely uses a different literary style:

> All are not apostles, are they? All are not prophets, are they? All are not teachers, are they? All are not workers of miracles, are they? All do not have gifts of healings, do they? All do not speak with tongues, do they? All do not interpret, do they?

The answer, obviously, is no; but Paul uses these rhetorical questions with another purpose in mind. He is building to the climax of verse 31a:

> But earnestly desire the greater gifts.

This phrase could actually be rendered, "All of you are striving for the showy gifts," as David Prior explains:

> Most English translations assume that the Greek verb, *zēloute,* is imperative: *earnestly desire the higher gifts.* It could well be indicative, *i.e.* stating as a fact that the Corinthians [were coveting] the higher gifts.[4]

---

4. David Prior, *The Message of 1 Corinthians,* The Bible Speaks Today Series (Downers Grove, Ill.: InterVarsity Press, 1985), p. 223.

73

Perhaps the Corinthians were coveting what they supposed were the "greater gifts"—miracles, healing, or speaking in tongues. They might have been, as Prior suggests, "prizing the more dramatic above the more ordinary."[5] So Paul stops to show them a "still more excellent way" (v. 31b)—the way of love in chapter 13.

When we reach chapter 14, we find that Paul has resumed his discussion of the gifts and narrowed his focus to one specific gift—tongues. In so doing, he evaluates its practice by comparing it to prophecy—which is proved to be the superior gift.

Prophecy Is Superior for the Insider

Prophets, remember, were inspired spokespeople for God, infallible messengers who revealed God's Word before the New Testament was finalized. Today we no longer need prophets. However, our modern-day equivalent to the gift of prophecy would be the ministry of the Word of God that takes place in our churches.

Prophecy, or the ministry of the Word, was superior to tongues for those inside the church for at least three basic reasons.

First: *Speaking in tongues doesn't edify the church, but the ministry of the Word does.* Paul gives a clear presentation of this in verses 2–5 of chapter 14.

> For one who speaks in a tongue does not speak to men, but to God; for no one understands, but in his spirit he speaks mysteries. But one who prophesies speaks to men for edification and exhortation and consolation. One who speaks in a tongue edifies himself; but one who prophesies edifies the church. Now I wish that you all spoke in tongues, but even more that you would prophesy; and greater is one who prophesies than one who speaks in tongues, unless he interprets, so that the church may receive edifying.

Second: *Speaking in tongues doesn't benefit the church without an interpreter, but the ministry of the Word does.* Verses 6–15 establish his second point.

> But now, brethren, if I come to you speaking in tongues, what shall I profit you, unless I speak to

5. Prior, *The Message of 1 Corinthians*, p. 223.

you either by way of revelation or of knowledge or of prophecy or of teaching?. . . Unless you utter by the tongue speech that is clear, how will it be known what is spoken? For you will be speaking into the air. . . . If then I do not know the meaning of the language, I shall be to the one who speaks a barbarian, and the one who speaks will be a barbarian to me. So also you, since you are zealous of spiritual gifts, seek to abound for the edification of the church. Therefore let one who speaks in a tongue pray that he may interpret. For if I pray in a tongue, my spirit prays, but my mind is unfruitful. What is the outcome then? I shall pray with the spirit and I shall pray with the mind also; I shall sing with the spirit and I shall sing with the mind also.

Third: *Speaking in tongues doesn't instruct the church, but the ministry of the Word does.* Paul's key statement in his evaluation of tongues comes in verse 19:

In the church I desire to speak five words with my mind, that I may instruct others also, rather than ten thousand words in a tongue.

The person speaking in tongues without interpretation can't present the Word of God as clearly as the one speaking the language the people understand. This fact makes the simple proclamation of Scripture more valuable, especially for those who are new to the church.

Prophecy Is Also Superior for the Outsider

Cutting through the cacophonous chaos of uninterpreted tongues is again the ministry of the Word, which brings composure and clarity to the church service so that the Holy Spirit can impact the non-Christian without obstruction.

If therefore the whole church should assemble together and all speak in tongues, and ungifted men or unbelievers enter, will they not say that you are mad? But if all prophesy, and an unbeliever or an ungifted man enters, he is convicted by all, he is called to account by all; the secrets of his heart are disclosed; and so he will fall on his face and worship

God, declaring that God is certainly among you.
(vv. 23–25)

Being a "two-edged sword," God's Word has the power to cut right to people's hearts, exposing secret sins and showing their need for Christ (see also Heb. 4:12). The Corinthians' misuse of tongues, though, weakened the effectiveness of God's Word, because unbelievers simply could not understand what was being spoken. So, to correct the problem, Paul gives important instructions on how to regain control of this gift.

The Regulation of Tongues: Principles to Remember

Through four main principles, Paul orchestrates the proper use of tongues in the overall flow of worship for the church in Corinth.

The Edification Principle

Speaking in tongues, along with other aspects of the worship service, should build up and enlighten those who hear it.

> When you assemble, each one has a psalm, has a teaching, has a revelation, has a tongue, has an interpretation. Let all things be done for edification. (v. 26b)

The Procedure Principle

Unfortunately, the Corinthians' worship was less than edifying because, like musicians tuning up before the conductor arrives, those with the gift of tongues all spoke at once. Assaulted by the dissonance of their unintelligible words and sounds, Paul covers his ears and says,

> If anyone speaks in a tongue, it should be by two or at the most three, and *each in turn.* (v. 27a, emphasis added)

The Interpretation Principle

Even if they were speaking in turn, though, how could those in the Corinthian church understand the mysterious messages? Paul says that someone with the gift of interpretation needed to translate (v. 27b). And if there was no interpreter?

> Let him keep silent in the church; and let him speak to himself and to God. (v. 28)

Besides giving us an important principle, this verse shows that those speaking in tongues could restrain their gift, keeping it to themselves so as not to detract from the worship service. Commentator David Prior reinforces this truth.

> Speaking in tongues . . . is not an uncontrollable phenomenon. The person with the gift can choose either to use it or not to use it. . . . For this reason it is very misleading to use such language as "ecstasy" . . . to describe any of the Spirit's gifts, but particularly speaking in tongues. Such terminology reintroduces pagan concepts and experiences into the arena of God's operations. His Spirit does not override the wills and minds of human beings. On the contrary, in his love he wins our willing cooperation, and he never forces us to do anything.[6]

The Humility/Orderly Principle

Apparently, the Corinthians also thought that they had a corner on spirituality—a bubble the apostle Paul soon burst.

> Was it from you that the word of God first went forth? Or has it come to you only? (v. 36)

What audacity to use the gifts God has given us to feed our egos instead of humbly using them in His service! So Paul, knowing that a fall soon follows pride (Prov. 16:18), protectively warns the Corinthian church to serve God in humility.

> If anyone thinks he is a prophet or spiritual, let him recognize that the things which I write to you are the Lord's commandment. But if anyone does not recognize this, he is not recognized. (vv. 37–38)

His final piece of advice comes in verses 39–40.

> Therefore, my brethren, desire earnestly to prophesy, and do not forbid to speak in tongues. But let all things be done properly and in an orderly manner.

6. Prior, *The Message of 1 Corinthians*, pp. 250–51.

A Final Word

This study of Paul's counsel on tongues certainly has a lot of information packed into it. To help keep the central focus in view, let's turn to William Barclay, who eloquently distills Paul's message for us.

> Paul comes near to the end of this section with some very practical advice. He is determined that anyone who possesses a gift should receive every chance to exercise it; but he is equally determined that the services of the Church should not become a kind of competitive disorder. . . . There must be liberty but there must be no disorder. The God of peace must be worshipped in peace.[7]

 ## Living Insights

Loving one another is easy when

you speak the same lingo,
    you enjoy the same worship,
        you believe the same teaching.

Loving one another is difficult when

        you speak a different lingo,
    you enjoy different worship,
you believe different teaching.

The true test of our Christianity is whether we can love others when it is difficult. And for many, loving is most difficult when it comes to the controversial spiritual gifts like speaking in tongues.

Choosing to love others in spite of our differences is the key to a life-giving church. And Paul shows us how to use this key in 1 Corinthians 13:4–8a. We've already spent some time with this passage in lesson 5, but today we're going to interact with it in another way. Think through the verses in light of their context—conflicts regarding spiritual gifts. This may reveal aspects of Paul's words you've never seen before.

---

7. William Barclay, *The Letters to the Corinthians*, rev. ed., The Daily Study Bible Series (Philadelphia, Pa.: Westminster Press, 1975), pp. 133–34.

Toward others who believe differently about tongues . . .

	Usually	Sometimes	Needs Work!
I am slow to lose patience	☐	☐	☐
I look for ways of being constructive	☐	☐	☐
I am not possessive	☐	☐	☐
I am not anxious to impress	☐	☐	☐
I do not cherish inflated ideas of my own importance	☐	☐	☐
I have good manners	☐	☐	☐
I do not pursue selfish advantage	☐	☐	☐
I am not touchy	☐	☐	☐
I do not keep account of evil	☐	☐	☐
I do not gloat over the wickedness of other people	☐	☐	☐
I share the joy of those who live by the truth	☐	☐	☐
I know no limits to my endurance	☐	☐	☐
I have no end to my trust	☐	☐	☐
I have no fading of my hope	☐	☐	☐
My love can outlast anything	☐	☐	☐
My love never fails[8]	☐	☐	☐

Based on this self-evaluation, which qualities of love are you having the most difficulty with?

_____

8. Based on J. B. Phillips' *The New Testament in Modern English*, rev. ed. (New York, N.Y.: Macmillan Publishing Co., 1972).

How can you begin changing your attitudes to reflect these qualities?

_____

_____

_____

🍇 Living Insights

As we saw in our lesson, one of the purposes of the gift of tongues was evangelism—"one beggar telling another where to find bread."[9]

We complicate this simple, life-giving exchange, however, when we use words the average unbeliever doesn't understand—like "born again," "rapture," or "vicarious atonement." Although one beggar may know where to find bread, the other beggar can't understand the directions to getting it—they might as well be speaking in a different tongue.

Suppose a friend who has never been to a Christian church before came to your church last Sunday. What words or experiences would have been difficult for your friend to understand?

_____

_____

The Corinthian church's services completely confused unbelievers (1 Cor. 14:23). What was Paul's solution to the problem (vv. 24–25)?

_____

_____

How do you think you and your church can more clearly communicate God's Word?

_____

_____

_____

9. D. T. Niles, as quoted by Bruce Larson in *Setting Men Free* (Grand Rapids, Mich.: Zondervan Publishing House, 1967), p. 41.

Chapter 10

HOW CAN I KNOW
MY SPIRITUAL GIFT?

1 Timothy 4:11–16

The Springfield, Oregon, *Public Schools Newsletter* once published an article describing what happens when we try to be someone we're not. Starring in this little parable are a duck, a rabbit, a squirrel, and an eagle.

Once upon a time, the animals decided they should do something meaningful to meet the problems of the new world. So they organized a school.

They adopted an activity curriculum of running, climbing, swimming and flying. To make it easier to administer the curriculum, all the animals took all the subjects.

The *duck* was excellent in swimming; in fact, better than his instructor. But he made only passing grades in flying, and was very poor in running. Since he was slow in running, he had to drop swimming and stay after school to practice running. This caused his web feet to be badly worn, so that he was only average in swimming. But average was quite acceptable, so nobody worried about that—except the duck.

The *rabbit* started at the top of his class in running, but developed a nervous twitch in his leg muscles because of so much make-up work in swimming.

The *squirrel* was excellent in climbing, but he encountered constant frustration in flying class because his teacher made him start from the ground up instead of from the treetop down. He developed "charlie horses" from overexertion, and so only got a C in climbing and a D in running.

The *eagle* was a problem child and was severely disciplined for being a non-conformist. In climbing

classes he beat all the others to the top of the tree,
but insisted on using his own way to get there.[1]

The moral of the story? Each of us has God-given abilities in
which we excel, and we shouldn't try filling a mold that doesn't
fit. A duck can't run like a rabbit, but neither can a rabbit swim
like a duck. So should the duck envy the rabbit or feel guilty
because it waddles during running class?

Yet how often do we envy others' gifts or feel ashamed because
we can't witness as effectively as an evangelist or minister as tenderly
as a mercy-giver? God has not made us all the same, but has designed us with different interests and skills. Why? Because He loves
variety, and the body needs it (see 1 Cor. 12:4–6, 27).

So if you're a duck, don't neglect your strengths—concentrate
on swimming. Essentially, this is what Paul is saying to his young
pastor friend Timothy.

Eight Words to Remember When Tempted to Stay Uninvolved

"Timothy . . ." You can almost hear fatherly Paul say his name.

Do not neglect the spiritual gift within you.
(1 Tim. 4:14a)

Literally, "Do not be careless with your spiritual gift; pay close
attention to it." Perhaps Timothy tended to be indifferent toward
it. Maybe he was caught up in the comparison game we sometimes
play, sizing up his abilities in relation to others'. So Paul reminds
him to refocus his energy on cultivating and using his own gift.

We, too, need to heed Paul's reminder to Timothy, watching
out for weeds of indifference in our own attitudes. But indifference
is not the only crabgrass in the garden. There are other attitudes
to beware of—attitudes that reflect an immaturity we often associ-
ate with the adolescent years.

Four Adolescent Attitudes to Watch Out For

A turned-up nose and a turned-down lower lip accompanied by
a foot stamp and a door slam are responses sometimes associated
with adolescence. If we're not careful, we can reflect similar behavior when it comes to using our spiritual gifts. Here are just a
few ways immaturity can surface.

1. As quoted by Charles R. Swindoll in *Standing Out*, 2d ed. (Portland, Oreg.: Multnomah
Press, 1983), p. 51.

First: *"I am waiting for a sudden inspiration from God; then I will exercise my gift."* It is tempting to wait for an emotionally-charged inspiration to ignite the use of our gift. But God doesn't send flaming arrows to point out the ministry for us. Rather, He uses a more commonsense process to help us decide where and when to get involved.

Second: *"My gift is the most important—or least important—of all."* One extreme is self-seeking and the other self-abasing, and both miss the mark entirely. For the Lord never ranks the gifts or the people who have them. All are necessary; therefore one gift is never more or less important than another (see 1 Cor. 12:18–25).

Third: *"I refuse all involvements except in the area of my gift."* The fact that more fruit grows in a ministry in which you are gifted doesn't mean that you should pull up roots in other ministries. Timothy was gifted as a pastor, but interestingly, Paul urged him to "do the work of an evangelist" (2 Tim. 4:5). Likewise, we should concentrate our efforts on our gift, but we can experience joy in serving the Lord in other areas too.

Fourth: *"I quit because of a conflict with someone/because of lack of appreciation."* When you work with people, conflicts will naturally occur. This is just a fact of life, and so is sometimes having to cope with the absence of affirmation. But conflicts and thankless responses are part and parcel of serving Christ, and if we let Him, He will use such times to build a priceless character within us.

As you start to find ways to get involved, be on the lookout for these four attitudes in your heart. Steering clear of them will make your search easier, and so will following five practical guidelines Paul offers in 1 Timothy 4:11–16.

Five Guidelines to Follow When Considering the Gifts

In the "Living Insights" throughout this study, you have had the opportunity to reflect on what your spiritual gift might be. As you continue following this path of discovery, keep in mind these words of advice that will serve as guideposts along the way.

Be Informed

Paul first counsels Timothy to "prescribe and teach these things" (1 Tim. 4:11). In other words, Paul is telling him to lay out the truth systematically and accurately. We are to take this same care with God's Word as we strive to be informed about the spiritual gifts.[2]

This study has been a part of your investigation, but it is only the beginning. Thoroughly search out information in a variety of resources, and continue to reflect on your own interests and aptitudes as you probe.

An important tool to carry with you is an inquisitive spirit. Avoid assuming you don't have a certain gift on the list without adequate questioning and contemplation. Be quiet. Be prayerful. Mostly, be open and tolerant—Paul's next words of advice.

Be Open and Tolerant

Apparently, Timothy had been closing himself off to certain ministries because of his age. So Paul writes,

> Let no one look down on your youthfulness, but
> rather in speech, conduct, love, faith and purity,
> show yourself an example of those who believe. (v. 12)

Paul is essentially saying, "Don't negate yourself; rather, be open to how God can use you." Similarly, we are to open our own horizons, being tolerant to the sometimes surprising ways God wants to use us.

You may say, "Oh, I can't teach!" "I can't help!" "What do I have to offer?" "I'm too young" or "too old" or "too inexperienced." That's negating yourself. God may have gifted you in ways you never thought possible. So experiment with different gifts. Tolerate new ideas and be open.

Be Attentive

In addition, Paul wisely advises Timothy,

> Until I come, give attention to the public reading
> of Scripture, to exhortation and teaching. (v. 13)

By giving his attention to Scripture, exhortation, and teaching, Timothy would be concentrating on his area of giftedness. As you pinpoint your own gift, focus your attention on several important evaluative factors.

Be attentive, first, to the *ease* with which you perform your gift; second, to your degree of spiritual *effectiveness*; third, to others'

---

2. Remember to pay particular attention to the passages dealing specifically with spiritual gifts: Romans 12, 1 Corinthians 12, Ephesians 4, 1 Peter 4.

reactions; and fourth, to your own *feelings.* And ask these kinds of questions: Did my efforts seem easy? Were they effective? Did others respond positively? Did I feel I was in my niche? Was I comfortable and fulfilled?

This self-evaluation will be a valuable indicator of which gift is yours. However, when you've finally nailed down your spiritual gift, don't put away the hammer yet. There's plenty more work to be done!

Be Diligent

> Take pains with these things; be absorbed in them,
> so that your progress may be evident to all. (v. 15)

"Take pains." "Be absorbed." Paul instructs his pupil to work diligently in the exercise of his gifts. Similarly, the fact that we are gifted doesn't mean that we can coast on our gift. After all, it takes chipping and cutting and polishing to make a diamond beautiful, and so it does with us.

Be Faithful

The Apostle wraps up his instruction to Timothy by admonishing,

> Pay close attention to yourself and to your teaching;
> persevere in these things. (v. 16a)

Exercising our gifts may require labor, but the results are worth it. So, as Paul encourages Timothy, "persevere"—be faithful. There is a lifetime of ministry ahead of you, more than just a few months in a Sunday school class or a term on a church board. Develop your gift for the long haul, and use it regularly.

Two Warnings to Heed When Exercising Your Gift(s)

Now that you're on the path to discovering and using your gift, take note of a couple of pitfalls along the way that could trip you up and hinder your ministry.

First: *Guard against the "I am indispensable" attitude.* As valuable as we are to the body of Christ, as significant as our gift is in God's plan for His church, we are never indispensable. Christ's work doesn't rise and fall with our presence and our gifts. On the contrary, He can accomplish His will through someone else as well as through us. So express your gift with a humble heart, understanding its limitations in addition to its values.

Second: *Check your motive.* The Corinthian believers failed to check their motives, and as a result, they abused their gifts. We can check the nature of our inner motives by simply asking the question *why.* Why did I give? Why did I lead? Why did I show mercy? Was I trying to shine my own light? Was I impelled by duty or guilt, or was it truly love?

A Concluding Thought

Prior to studying the spiritual gifts, your efforts in ministry may have resembled a duck in a footrace or a rabbit on a swim team. As a result, you may be less than enthusiastic about getting involved today. But if our study has encouraged you to do anything, let it be this: Take a risk.

You *can* discover your spiritual gift, but it means taking a chance, trying new ministries, saying yes although you've said no up until now. It means determining to be the person God has designed you to be.

When you find that niche with your name on it, you'll exclaim, "This is it!" Because finally, you'll be filling a mold . . . that fits.

 Living Insights   STUDY ONE

Visiting someone in the hospital, explaining the gospel to a stranger, giving twice as much as usual, or leading the children's choir are all expressions of one spiritual gift or another. And they all involve risk—particularly if they are first-time experiences.

How can we build confidence when we are discovering our gift and stepping out into the unknown? Perhaps a vignette from Frederick Buechner's book *The Wizard's Tide* can point us to an answer.

Mr. Schroeder has decided that his son, Teddy, is old enough to swim out with him to some barrels anchored a ways offshore. Halfway to the barrels, Teddy starts getting nervous.

> Teddy thought the barrels still looked a long way off, and the beach was so far behind he could hardly recognize his mother and Bean [Teddy's sister] sitting on it. His arms were beginning to ache, and he was feeling out of breath. What if he started to drown, he thought? What if he called for help and his father, who was a little ahead of him, didn't hear? What if

a giant octopus swam up from below and wrapped him in its slimy green tentacles?

But just as he was thinking these things, his father turned around and treaded water, waiting for him. "How about a lift the rest of the way?" Mr. Schroeder said. So Teddy paddled over and put his arms around his father's neck from behind, and that was the best part of the day for him and the part he remembered for many years afterward. . . .

His mother said bad things about his father. She said that he had no get-up-and-go and that he was worse than Grandpa Schroeder already though thirty years younger. She said he needed a swift kick in the pants and things like that. And Teddy knew that his father did things that he wished he wouldn't, like drink too many cocktails and drive his car up on the lawn and come to kiss him and Bean good-night with his face all clammy and cold.

But as he swam out toward the barrels on his father's back, he also knew that there was no place in the whole Atlantic ocean where he felt so safe.[3]

This image of a boy clinging onto his daddy's shoulders aptly portrays the kind of dependence on the Lord we need when trying new ministries. If Teddy felt secure trusting in his often-failing father, how much more should we feel confident in our never-failing Lord? Surely, there is no other place in the whole world where we can feel so safe.

 Living Insights STUDY TWO

Take a moment to look back at what you wrote in Study One of the first chapter's "Living Insights." You were asked to take a guess at what your spiritual gift might be. Having worked through the rest of the study and filled out the other "Living Insights," has your opinion changed? What gift or gifts do you now think you might have?

3. Frederick Buechner, *The Wizard's Tide* (San Francisco, Calif.: Harper and Row, Publishers, 1990), pp. 45–46.

_____

_____

_____

Why do you think you might have this gift?

_____

_____

In what ministries can you express this gift?

_____

_____

As you experiment with your gift, trying it in different ministries, remember the advice from this last lesson:

- Be informed about the spiritual gifts, particularly yours.
- Be open and tolerant to the possible ways God has gifted you.
- Be attentive to the signs that He is using you.
- Be diligent in building your gift to its highest potential.
- Be faithful by regularly expressing your gift.

◆

Heavenly Father,

You have placed in my hands this precious gift. Help me to use it confidently, knowing that it is Your Spirit who empowers us. Help me to use it humbly, knowing that I received it purely by grace. Help me to use it lovingly, knowing that by how I use it, others will shape their understanding of You.

Here. Now I return Your gift—but in a different form. My feet, my hands, my voice, my mind, my all I offer back to You. Your gift in me; my gift to You. Amen.

BOOKS FOR
PROBING FURTHER

It would be difficult to state the essential truths concerning spiritual gifts as succinctly and powerfully as Arthur T. Pierson, who wrote:

> Everyone has some gift, therefore all should be encouraged.
> No one has all gifts, therefore all should be humble.
> All gifts are for the one Body, therefore all should be harmonious.
> All gifts are from the Lord, therefore all should be contented.
> All gifts are mutually helpful and needful, therefore all should be studiously faithful.
> All gifts promote the health and strength of the whole Body, therefore none can be safely dispensed with.
> All gifts depend on His fulness for power, therefore all should keep in close touch with Him.[1]

Pierson's statements are right on target. Understanding and using our gifts is not just an intellectual exercise; rather it is a vital aspect of our total spiritual well-being.

It is our hope that this study will be just the beginning of a lifelong journey for you—a journey and an exploration of the far-reaching implications of spiritual gifts. To help you take the next step of your adventure, we've compiled a list of resources that will give you guidance and insight. Godspeed!

The Holy Spirit

Packer, J. I. *Keep In Step with the Spirit.* Old Tappan, N.J.: Fleming H. Revell Co., 1984. Providing an excellent overview of the Holy

---

1. Arthur T. Pierson, as quoted by J. Oswald Sanders in *The Holy Spirit and His Gifts*, rev. and enl. (Grand Rapids, Mich.: Zondervan Publishing House, 1970), p. 115.

Spirit's ministry in the believer's life, this volume also includes a thoughtful and well-balanced analysis of the charismatic movement.

Ryrie, Charles Caldwell. *The Holy Spirit.* Chicago, Ill.: Moody Press, 1965. This classic resource provides a broad view of scriptural teaching on the Holy Spirit and also focuses on His ministry today.

Spiritual Gifts in General

Gangel, Kenneth O. *Unwrap Your Spiritual Gifts.* Wheaton, Ill.: SP Publications, Victor Books, 1983. From "administration" to "wisdom," this book covers each gift using sound biblical interpretation. It is an excellent starting point for studying the spiritual gifts.

McRae, William. *Dynamics of Spiritual Gifts.* Grand Rapids, Mich.: Zondervan Publishing House, 1976. Probing issues such as the definition, distribution, description, distinctions, discovery, and development of spiritual gifts, the author provides a detailed and thorough treatment of the subject.

Thomas, Robert L. *Understanding Spiritual Gifts.* Chicago, Ill.: Moody Press, 1978. Thomas digs deeply into 1 Corinthians 12–14, offering serious students a detailed examination of this challenging section of Scripture and the subject of spiritual gifts.

The Support Gifts

Anderson, Robert C. *The Effective Pastor.* Chicago, Ill.: Moody Press, 1985. Anderson is a pastor's pastor and counsels those with this gift about how to know their calling; how to organize their personal, family, and clerical life; and how to meet the day-to-day demands of the ministry.

Petersen, Jim. *Living Proof.* Colorado Springs, Colo.: NavPress, 1989. From an analysis of our times to helpful tips on taking the first steps of sharing your faith, the author lays out all the equipment you'll need to effectively evangelize. This book is a must-read even for those who don't have the gift of evangelism.

Wilhoit, Jim, and Leland Ryken. *Effective Bible Teaching.* Grand Rapids, Mich.: Baker Book House, 1988. Colleagues on the faculty of Wheaton College, the authors offer expert insights into study, preparation, and classroom techniques that are sure to develop your gift of teaching.

The Service Gifts

Bayly, Joseph. *The Last Thing We Talk About.* Revised edition. Elgin, Ill.: David C. Cook Publishing Co., 1973. Having suffered the painful loss of three of his children, Bayly gives you a guided tour through the mourning process so that you can fully understand how to show mercy to those in need.

Bright, Bill. *Believing God for the Impossible.* San Bernardino, Calif.: Here's Life Publishers, Campus Crusade for Christ International, 1979. Authored by a man with unsinkable faith, this book will inspire you to do as he has done—believe God for the impossible and watch it happen.

Crabb, Lawrence J., Jr., and Dan B. Allender. *Encouragement: The Key to Caring.* Grand Rapids, Mich.: Zondervan Publishing House, Pyranee Books, 1984. This work on how to encourage someone "to be a better Christian, even when life is rough" is an exhorter's handbook. It will teach you when to tell someone how you feel, how to use encouragement opportunities, and even what to say and how to say it!

Ford, Leighton. *Transforming Leadership.* Downers Grove, Ill.: InterVarsity Press, 1991. Looking to Jesus as a model, Ford constructs what it takes to be a leader in today's world. His principles come out of a rich experience in leadership training and will shape you into an effective agent for change in your church and community.

LeTourneau, R. G. *Mover of Men and Mountains.* Englewood Cliffs, N.J.: Prentice-Hall, 1960. Possessing the gift of giving, LeTourneau, a successful inventor and engineer, often donated 90 percent of his income to the Lord's work. He will amaze you with his pioneering spirit and generous heart.

Swindoll, Charles R. *Improving Your Serve.* Dallas, Tex.: Word Publishing, 1981. Subtitled "The Art of Unselfish Living," this book will encourage you to use your abilities to serve others. His model is Jesus, our God who knelt to wash His disciples' feet.

The Sign Gifts

Barron, Bruce. *The Health and Wealth Gospel.* Downers Grove, Ill.: InterVarsity Press, 1987. With chapter titles that pose to-the-point questions such as "Does God Want You Healthy?" and "Does the Bible Really Say That?", the author offers an insightful analysis of the popular "name it, claim it" theology of some charismatic teachers.

Edgar, Thomas R. *Miraculous Gifts: Are They for Today?* Neptune, N.J.: Loizeaux Brothers, 1983. This treatise zeroes in on prophecy, apostleship, miracles, healing, and tongues, presenting a convincing case for the cessation of these gifts. The author also includes appendices on the service and support gifts that are in use today.

Horton, Michael, ed. *The Agony of Deceit.* Chicago, Ill.: Moody Press, 1990. Horton features authors such as R. C. Sproul and Joel Nederhood, who pull back the curtain and expose the unbiblical practices and teachings used by some televangelists. C. Everett Koop's chapter, "Faith-Healing and the Sovereignty of God," alone is worth the price of the book.

Some of the books listed here may be out of print and available only through a library. All of these works are recommended reading only. With the exception of books by Charles R. Swindoll, none of them are available through Insight for Living. If you wish to obtain some of these suggested readings, please contact your local Christian bookstore.

ORDERING INFORMATION

Cassette Tapes and Study Guide

This Bible study guide was designed to be used independently or in conjunction with the broadcast of Chuck Swindoll's taped messages on the topic listed below. If you would like to order cassette tapes or further copies of this study guide, please see the information given below and the Order Form provided on the last page of this guide.

HE GAVE GIFTS

In serving the Lord, have you ever felt out of your niche? Uncomfortable? Often ready to quit? God created within each of His children certain abilities—spiritual gifts—that enable us to function in the body of Christ with *effectiveness* and *ease*. Through this study, hopefully, you will begin to discover your own personal gifts. And once you become involved in effectively ministering to others through the exercise of those gifts, you're sure to feel right at home with your life because you'll be filling a mold . . . that fits!

			Calif.*	U.S.	B.C.*	Canada*
HGG	CS	Cassette series, includes album cover	$31.64	$29.50	$45.01	$42.76
HGG	1–5	Individual cassettes, include messages A and B	5.36	5.00	7.61	7.23
HGG	SG	Study Guide	4.24	3.95	5.08	5.08

*These prices already include the following charges: for delivery in **California,** applicable sales tax; **Canada,** 7% GST and 7% postage and handling (on tapes only); **British Columbia,** 7% GST, 6% British Columbia sales tax (on tapes only), and 7% postage and handling (on tapes only). **The prices are subject to change without notice.**

HGG 1-A: *He Gave Gifts*—Selected Scripture
    B: *Gifts That Grab Our Attention*—1 Corinthians 12:14–27; Ephesians 4:11–13
HGG 2-A: *The Pastor-Teacher, the Teacher . . . and the Taught*—Selected Scripture
    B: *A Salute to the Servers*—Romans 12:1–7; 1 Corinthians 12:28

HGG 3-A: *Gifts Most Mothers Model*—Selected Scripture
   B: *Unidentical Twins in the Same Body*—Romans 12:3–8;
   1 Corinthians 12:7–9
HGG 4-A: *What About Miracles and Healing Today?*—
   Acts 3:1–16
   B: *A Calm, Scriptural Analysis of Healing*—
   1 Corinthians 12:10, 28–30; James 5:13–16
HGG 5-A: *The Gift of Speaking in Tongues*—Acts 2:1–11;
   1 Corinthians 14
   B: *How Can I Know My Spiritual Gift?*—1 Timothy 4:11–16

How to Order by Mail

Simply mark on the order form whether you want the series or individual tapes. Mail the form with your payment to the appropriate address listed below. We will process your order as promptly as we can.

United States: Mail your order to the Sales Department at Insight for Living, Post Office Box 69000, Anaheim, California 92817-0900. If you wish your order to be shipped first-class for faster delivery, add 10 percent of the total order amount. Otherwise, please allow four to six weeks for delivery by fourth-class mail. We accept personal checks, money orders, Visa, or MasterCard in payment for materials. Unfortunately, we are unable to offer invoicing or COD orders.

Canada: Mail your order to Insight for Living Ministries, Post Office Box 2510, Vancouver, British Columbia V6B 3W7. Allow approximately four weeks for delivery. We accept personal checks, money orders, Visa, or MasterCard in payment for materials. Unfortunately, we are unable to offer invoicing or COD orders.

Australia, New Zealand, or Papua New Guinea: Mail your order to Insight for Living, Inc., GPO Box 2823 EE, Melbourne, Victoria 3001, Australia. Please allow six to ten weeks for delivery by surface mail. If you would like your order sent airmail, the delivery time may be reduced. Using the United States price as a base, add postage costs—surface or airmail—to the amount of your order. Please use the chart that follows to determine correct postage. Due to fluctuating currency rates, we can accept only personal checks made payable in U.S. funds, international money orders, Visa, or MasterCard in payment for materials.

Overseas: In other international locations, residents should mail their orders to our United States office. Please allow six to ten weeks for delivery by surface mail. If you would like your order sent airmail, the delivery time may be reduced. Using the United States price as a base, add postage costs—surface or airmail—to the amount of your order. Please use the chart that follows to determine correct postage. Due to fluctuating currency rates, we can accept only personal checks made payable in U.S. funds, international money orders, Visa, or MasterCard in payment for materials.

Type of Postage	Postage Cost
Surface	10% of total order
Airmail	25% of total order

For Faster Service, Order by Telephone or FAX

For Visa or MasterCard orders, you are welcome to use one of our toll-free numbers between the hours of 7:00 A.M. and 4:30 P.M., Pacific time, Monday through Friday, or our FAX numbers. The numbers to use from anywhere in the United States are **1-800-772-8888** or FAX (714) 575-5049. To order from Canada, call our Vancouver office using **1-800-663-7639** or FAX (604) 596-2975. Vancouver residents, call (604) 596-2910. Australian residents should phone (03) 872-4606. From other international locations, call our Sales Department at (714) 575-5000 in the United States.

Our Guarantee

Our cassettes are guaranteed for ninety days against faulty performance or breakage due to a defect in the tape. For best results, please be sure your tape recorder is in good operating condition and is cleaned regularly.

Note: To cover processing and handling, there is a $10 fee for *any* returned check.

Insight for Living Catalog

Request a free copy of the Insight for Living catalog of books, tapes, and study guides by calling **1-800-772-8888** in the United States or **1-800-663-7639** in Canada.

Order Form

HGG CS represents the entire *He Gave Gifts* series in a special album cover, while HGG 1–5 are the individual tapes included in the series. HGG SG represents this study guide, should you desire to order additional copies.

Item	Calif.*	Unit Price U.S.	B.C.*	Canada*	Quantity	Amount
HGG CS	$31.64	$29.50	$45.01	$42.76		$
HGG 1	5.36	5.00	7.61	7.23		
HGG 2	5.36	5.00	7.61	7.23		
HGG 3	5.36	5.00	7.61	7.23		
HGG 4	5.36	5.00	7.61	7.23		
HGG 5	5.36	5.00	7.61	7.23		
HGG SG	4.24	3.95	5.08	5.08		
					Subtotal	
		Overseas Residents Pay U.S. price plus 10% surface postage or 25% airmail. Also, see "How to Order by Mail."				
		U.S. First-Class Shipping For faster delivery, add 10% for postage and handling.				
		Gift to Insight for Living Tax-deductible in the United States and Canada.				
					Total Amount Due Please do not send cash.	$

If there is a balance: ☐ Apply it as a donation ☐ Please refund
*These prices already include applicable taxes and shipping costs.

Payment by: ☐ Check or money order made payable to Insight for Living or

☐ Credit card (circle one): Visa MasterCard Number _____

Expiration Date _____ Signature _____
We cannot process your credit card purchase without your signature.

Name _____

Address _____

City _____ State/Province _____

Zip/Postal Code _____ Country _____

Telephone ( ) _____ Radio Station ___ ___ ___ ___
If questions arise concerning your order, we may need to contact you.

Mail this order form to the Sales Department at one of these addresses:
Insight for Living, Post Office Box 69000, Anaheim, CA 92817-0900
Insight for Living Ministries, Post Office Box 2510, Vancouver, BC, Canada V6B 3W7
Insight for Living, Inc., GPO Box 2823 EE, Melbourne, VIC 3001, Australia

Order Form

HGG CS represents the entire *He Gave Gifts* series in a special album cover, while HGG 1–5 are the individual tapes included in the series. HGG SG represents this study guide, should you desire to order additional copies.

Item	Calif.*	Unit Price U.S.	B.C.*	Canada*	Quantity	Amount
HGG CS	$31.64	$29.50	$45.01	$42.76		$
HGG 1	5.36	5.00	7.61	7.23		
HGG 2	5.36	5.00	7.61	7.23		
HGG 3	5.36	5.00	7.61	7.23		
HGG 4	5.36	5.00	7.61	7.23		
HGG 5	5.36	5.00	7.61	7.23		
HGG SG	4.24	3.95	5.08	5.08		
					Subtotal	
		Overseas Residents *Pay U.S. price plus 10% surface postage or 25% airmail. Also, see "How to Order by Mail."*				
		U.S. First-Class Shipping *For faster delivery, add 10% for postage and handling.*				
		Gift to Insight for Living *Tax-deductible in the United States and Canada.*				
					Total Amount Due *Please do not send cash.*	$

If there is a balance: ☐ Apply it as a donation ☐ Please refund
*These prices already include applicable taxes and shipping costs.

Payment by: ☐ Check or money order made payable to Insight for Living or

☐ Credit card (circle one): Visa MasterCard Number _____

Expiration Date _____ Signature _____
We cannot process your credit card purchase without your signature.

Name _____

Address _____

City _____ State/Province _____

Zip/Postal Code _____ Country _____

Telephone _(____)_____ Radio Station ___ ___ ___ ___
If questions arise concerning your order, we may need to contact you.

Mail this order form to the Sales Department at one of these addresses:
Insight for Living, Post Office Box 69000, Anaheim, CA 92817-0900
Insight for Living Ministries, Post Office Box 2510, Vancouver, BC, Canada V6B 3W7
Insight for Living, Inc., GPO Box 2823 EE, Melbourne, VIC 3001, Australia